Rapid Reading Practices

Developing Word Automaticity in Reading

KEITH S. FOLSE

University of Central Florida

Ann Arbor
The University of Michigan Press

2010   2009   2008   2007   4   3   2   1

ISBN-13: 978-0-472-03276-1
ISBN-10: 0-472-03276-3

Contents

To the Teacher

Rapid Reading Practices consists of 100 timed word practices. These practices cover words at four levels: basic, beginning, intermediate, and advanced. All readers can benefit from word recognition practice with even the most basic words because our goal is to increase readers' automaticity. Reading speed is dependent on how rapidly, or automatically, readers are able to recognize words, but learners are rarely given opportunities to practice word automaticity. Lack of vocabulary knowledge is a problem across all skill areas but is especially apparent in ESL reading. Eskey (1988) found that not being able to recognize the meaning of English words automatically causes students who are good readers in their native language to do excessive guesswork in the second language and that this guessing slows down the process of reading.

Of all the language skills, reading proficiency varies more from learner to learner. All students can improve their reading proficiency, including reading rate, and consistent and plentiful practice is essential. To maximize learners' improvement in reading rate, teachers must ensure that each learner completes all 100 of the practice exercises in this book. We recommend that learners do three to five exercises per day. Such a reading regimen means that this book will last 20 to 30 class meetings.

Improving Reading Speed

After general reading comprehension, perhaps the most serious problem encountered by developing readers is reading speed or reading rate. This might be true for many reasons. The most likely culprit here is students' lack of reading automaticity—that is, their inability to recognize discrete vocabulary items rapidly. When readers are forced to decode a frequent word every time they encounter it, they waste valuable time and cognition that could be devoted to reading comprehension instead of mere word recognition. Practicing automaticity allows readers to free up cognition that can be dedicated to higher-order thinking skills in reading.

Good readers have good vocabulary knowledge. While neither "causes" the other, we know that they are intricately related. Students must work toward expanding their vocabulary knowledge through explicit practice with words and through both intensive and extensive reading. Low reading rates could be due to the tendency of some readers to fixate too long on unknown words instead of continuing to attempt the reading. The timed word selection exercises will work on this problem.

Book Organization

- The **basic level** consists of Exercises 1–25, which include words from the Dolch List.
- The **beginning level** consists of Exercises 26–40, which include very frequent words.
- The **intermediate level** consists of Exercises 41–70, which include frequent words.
- The **advanced level** consists of Exercises 71–100, which include words from the Academic Word List (AWL).

Exercises 1–25 (Basic Level) include words from the Dolch List. These 25 exercises have been arranged by pre-primer (Exercises 1–5), primer (Exercises 6–10), first grade (Exercises 11–15), second grade (Exercises 16–20), and third grade (Exercises 21–25). However, the use of *grade* here is not meant to imply that these words are necessary for children only; rather this use relates to level to help adults who need to improve automaticity.

The Dolch List was prepared by E.W. Dolch in 1936. The words in this list are high-frequency words that make up from 50 to 75 percent of the reading material in English in U.S. elementary schools. Because these words are so important to basic reading, all learners—not just children—need to recognize them automatically; hence, they are often called **sight words.** These words cannot be learned through use of pictures (there are no concrete nouns on the list); children must be able to recognize these words at a glance before they can read confidently. By the end of third grade, all English-speaking students should be able to recognize the 220 words on the Dolch List.

Exercises 26–70 practice frequently encountered words, including many words from the General Service List (GSL) (West 1953). The GSL is a list of 2,000 words whose frequency of occurrence make them of the greatest service to learners, hence the name for this list. The General Service List was widely used for years in designing content of graded readers and other learning materials. Exercises 26–40 (Beginning Level) practice words of higher frequency than those in Exercises 41–70 (Intermediate Level).

Exercises 71–100 (Advanced Level) practice advanced words from the Academic Word List (AWL). The 570 word families in the AWL (Coxhead 1998, 2000) were chosen through a rigorous selection process in which the words had to occur in more than half of the 28 subject areas in the academic corpus of 3,500,000 words from which the word families were pulled. In addition, words had to occur more than 100 times in the corpus, and words had to occur at least ten times in each of the subject areas. These guidelines produced a list of words that are useful for the widest possible range of both native and non-native learners of English. In reflecting the academic nature of this list, the AWL does not include any of the word families occurring in the General Service List.

A Comparison of Word Lists		
List	**Words**	**Notes**
Dolch List	220 sight words that elementary school children must be able to recognize	• Prepared in 1936 • Based on frequency • Mostly function words; does not include concrete words • Useful in K–3 reading materials
General Service List	2,000 words that are of general service to learners	• Published in 1953 • Based on frequency
Academic Word List	570 word families that occur in a variety of academic text materials	• Published in 1998 • Based on frequency • Only words that occur in many different types of academic material

From *Vocabulary Myths: Applying Second Language Research to Classroom Teaching* (p. 42), by Keith S. Folse, 2004, Ann Arbor: University of Michigan Press.

Timed Word Selection Exercises

In these exercises, students must read a word or group of words to the left and then find that same answer in a group of five options that look similar. For example, the students must circle the words *two* in the first example, *for you and* in the second, and *then she* in the last.

1. two	the	(two)	ten	too	twin
2. for you and	for me and	for us and	for him and	for her and	(for you and)
3. then she	then he	when she	(then she)	when he	then we

The goals of these exercises are to train students' eye movements in a left-to-right pattern and to provide practice recognizing similarly shaped letters and letter combinations. The four distractors contain letters that have similar shapes such as *b* and *d* or *ei* and *ie* and are therefore confusing to learners.

To improve reading speed, these exercises should be timed, thus encouraging students to work as rapidly as possible. It is recommended that teachers give students **30 seconds** to complete the 25 items in these exercises. Students should then correct their answers. Since it is difficult for students to catch their own errors in this kind of proofreading exercise, it is recommended that students exchange exercises and check each other's work to ensure accurate correcting. For each incorrect answer, students lose one correct answer. This penalty will encourage students to work carefully as well as rapidly. Afterward, students should record the number of correct answers on their progress charts (see pages 103–8). The maximum number of correct items per exercise is 25, so students scores could range from 0 to 25. However, actual classroom use of these materials shows that most students achieve an initial score of 14 to 20 items from the very beginning of the program, and scores gradually increase to near 25. Even when students may appear to have peaked, the consistent and plentiful practice will reinforce reading rate improvement.

In Exercises 1–70, the focus is on short, very frequent words. To improve automaticity, readers need to practice recognizing these words individually as well as in combination with other words. To this end, the 25 items in Exercises 1–70 contain 15–17 single words (e.g., *say*) and 8–10 multi-word items of two words (e.g., *I say*) or three words (e.g., *to live with*). Some multi-word items represent obvious units from a sentence (e.g., *one of the* or *He took the*), but other phrases that may appear less transparent are actually parts of a real sentence (e.g., *any in,* as in "The police searched for the money, but they did not find *any in* the vault").

In Exercises 71–100, the words from the Academic Word List are much longer and are therefore practiced individually. These 30 exercises contain 750 target words (to the left of the vertical line). The AWL arranges words in frequency bands from 1 (very frequent) to 10 (frequent). Words from Band 1 appear as target words five times. Words from Band 2 appear as target words four times. Words from Bands 3, 4, and 5 appear as target words one time. A small number of words from Band 6 were chosen to complete the 750 target words. However, all AWL words appear in the distractors to the right of the vertical line. Thus, learners will have to interact with all of the AWL words in these automaticity drills.

To be certain, reading rate is an important reading skill, but reading depends on a host of skills. For practice with a wider array of reading skills, including reading rate at both the word and the paragraph level, teachers should look at the third edition of *Intermediate Reading Practices* (Folse, 2004b) and *Beginning Reading Practices* (Folse, 1996).

Progress Charts

Students (and teachers) need to see a record of progress. The instructions for completing these charts can be found on page 103.

BIBLIOGRAPHY

Coxhead, A. (1998). *An academic word list.* English Language Institute Occasional Publication, Number 18. Wellington: Victoria University of Wellington.

Coxhead, A. (2000). A new academic word list. *TESOL Quarterly 34* (2), 213–238.

Eskey, D. (1988). Holding in the bottom: An interactive approach to the language problems of second language readers. In P. Carrell, J. Deveine, and D. Eskey, (Eds.), *Interactive approaches to second language reading* (pp. 3–23). Cambridge: Cambridge University Press.

Folse, K. (1996). *Beginning reading practices: Building reading and vocabulary strategies.* Ann Arbor: University of Michigan Press.

Folse, K. (2004a). *Intermediate reading practices: Building reading and vocabulary skills, 3d edition.* Ann Arbor: University of Michigan Press.

Folse, K. (2004b). *Vocabulary myths: Applying second language research to classroom teaching.* Ann Arbor: University of Michigan Press.

West, M. (1953). *A general service list of English words.* London: Longman.

Directions for All Exercises

Directions: Read the word or group of words to the left of the line. Then read the five words or group of words to the right. Circle the word that is exactly the same as the word or words to the left of the line.

◼ Exercise 1. Dolch: Pre-Primer

1. in	it	is	in	on	if
2. two	the	two	ten	too	twin
3. for you and	for me and	for you and	for us and	for him and	for her and
4. funny	fun for	fun is	funny	fun and	fun or
5. finding	finds	I find	we find	find	finding
6. here	here	hear	her	were	there
7. makes	makes	make	making	made	male
8. away	a way	my way	way	away	the way
9. where	were	we're	when	where	which
10. help	helps	help	helped	helping	helper
11. see	the	them	seed	sees	see
12. come	come	came	comes	cone	cones
13. it is	if it	is it	it is	it's	this
14. one big	one bag	one bed	one beg	one dig	one big
15. we can not	we can't	we can	weekend	we can not	we can note
16. you help	you have	you take	you help	you need	you like
17. my	my	me	more	am	by
18. I said	I say	I made	I have	I take	I said
19. blue and	and blue	blue and	and run	run and	the blue
20. you	your	young	yes	you	jump
21. little	litter	little	look	turtle	title
22. the one	the only	one of	not one	find one	the one
23. we play	we play	the play	I play	he plays	they play
24. to go	we go	to do	I go	to go	to be
25. runs	running	run	runs	ran	sun

Exercise 2. Dolch: Pre-Primer

1. go	do	go	be	am	is
2. red	red	ready	deer	dear	read
3. is	it	it is	is	is it	sit
4. up	up	off	on	at	down
5. make	make	makes	made	male	cake
6. I said	I say	I stay	I made	I said	I send
7. look	luck	looks	leaks	lock	look
8. to jump	to jump	to guess	together	to gather	to get
9. little	title	little	leather	lighter	titles
10. away	I may	a way	the way	go away	away
11. we	we	me	knee	see	be
12. it runs	it's a room	rit an	it runs	I run	I rent
13. where is	where	when is	where is	when	where's
14. down	done	down	doing	does	town
15. it is	this is	this	it's	it was	it is
16. and is funny	and is a fan	and is fun	and isn't fun	and is funny	and is a funny
17. I	a	i	A	I	E
18. åhere are	there are	they are	hear are	here are	here's
19. and it	and is	it, and	is, and	and it's	and it
20. said	says	said	soda	send	salt
21. blue	blow	bless	bulb	belt	blue
22. up	us	cup	up	mop	ad
23. the big	a big	the big	a bag	the bag	many big
24. we play	you pray	you play	we pray	we play	your player
25. can	loan	car	cat	can	can't

Exercise 3. Dolch: Pre-Primer

1. my three	me there	my thing	my thirsty	~~my three~~	my thread
2. jump	~~jump~~	joke	jeans	jam	jack
3. two	tow	twin	~~two~~	too	tea
4. I go	~~I go~~	I am	I'm going	I do	we go
5. where	were	~~where~~	we're	we are	wear
6. see	sea	sees	seed	bee	~~see~~
7. the big	the bag	the bug	the hug	~~the big~~	the bags
8. you find	you found	~~you find~~	we found	we find	your fan
9. helps	help	helping	helped	she helps	~~helps~~
10. one is	mine is	this is	one and	one of us	~~one is~~
11. you look	it looks	your book	you took	your books	~~you look~~
12. not	note	nut	~~not~~	ton	not
13. funny	my fun	found	fun for	~~funny~~	fin on
14. up	~~up~~	if	at	on	of
15. to	too	~~to~~	at	on	two
16. it can	~~it can~~	it's a cane	it can't	it cannot	it came
17. play	played	plays	~~play~~	player	plate
18. red	read	ready	real	~~red~~	raw
19. it is in	~~it is in~~	it is on	it's in	it's on	isn't it
20. here	there	~~here~~	hear	hour	her
21. for	tour	four	door	far	~~for~~
22. comes	~~cones~~	comes	cone	come	scam
23. make	cake	take	~~make~~	bake	rake
24. me	men	meet	am	me	ant
25. little	title	cattle	little	letter	better

Exercise 4. Dolch: Pre-Primer

1. the can	the cans	the cent	the can	the cents	they cannot
2. yellow	jello	you'll	yelling	yellow	elbow
3. I run	I ran	I run	I can	I rob	I rent
4. finds	finds	found	find	finding	finder
5. little	letter	title	better	little	last
6. down	dawn	down	wind	door	lawn
7. blue and	below and	true and	blond and	blue and	bend and
8. said	same	said	says	salt	soil
9. where	we're	when	where	whenever	wherever
10. is not	is not	is a note	isn't	note is	is for
11. funny	funny	fan of	found	honey	lovely
12. you	use	young	you're	you	your
13. away	a way	the way	my way	he may	away
14. him help	him helps	him helped	him help	him helper	him helping
15. and a	and an	and any	and one	and air	and a
16. here	here	there	heart	her	herself
17. it goes	it does	it mops	it's golf	it gains	it goes
18. one	on	on the	only	one	one of
19. three	three	these	those	them	trees
20. we	me	we	see	be	zoo
21. and two	and toes	and tow	and won't	and twins	and two
22. runs	tons	rivers	runs	river	run
23. my	me	men	man	by	my
24. a big	my bag	a big	a bag	a bad	a bag
25. for two	for twins	for them	for two	four, too	for the

■ *Exercise 5. Dolch: Pre-Primer*

1. little red	red letter	little road	little red	lemon drink	letter and
2. is	it	his	is	he's	it's
3. yellow	yell	other	gallon	below	yellow
4. up	up	under	pill	of	on
5. me	we	me	my	am	I'm
6. red	red	dear	ready	deer	rot
7. jumps	jumps	jump	jumped	jumper	jumping
8. go in	go on	go to	go by	go in	go an
9. plays	days	spray	lays	pays	plays
10. help me	to help me	help me	my help	helping me	my hope
11. come	coming	came	comes	cone	come
12. to the	to them	to those	to a	to the	to my
13. and not	am not	and not	are not	do not	or not
14. here	share	there	here	fear	clear
15. a little	a letter	a title	a leaf	a little	a dead
16. help	hope	hop	help	hello	hell
17. big	big	beg	bag	bug	dig
18. said	suit	sail	sale	salad	said
19. sees	seas	sees	seed	meet	says
20. and I	and me	and an	and I	and she	and then
21. down	town	down	done	tour	debt
22. three and	trees and	those and	these and	three and	them and
23. up	of	under	down	us	up
24. looked	looks	looking	booked	looked	booking
25. make	make	made	male	maker	matter

Exercise 6. Dolch: Primer

1. ran one	ran on	run on	run one	ran one	one run
2. four	found	for	fire	fear	four
3. what	who	when	where	which	what
4. did	did	does	do	done	died
5. eats	teas	eats	seat	tear	rates
6. went	want	wind	wax	weak	went
7. this	to his	it is	this is	it's this	this
8. out	our	tour	wrong	out	oats
9. good	body	wood	guide	gold	good
10. they are	they were	there are	they are	they aren't	the yard
11. at a	at one	ate a	at a	eat a	at an
12. on our	on our	in our	at out	off our	us our
13. please	please	pays	peas	possible	plays
14. must	most	must	mist	summer	I must
15. she	her	she	she's	he	he's
16. that is	that is	these are	this is	it's a hat	that's my
17. new	now	new	knew	know	when
18. what do	what does	when does	that does	what do	what did
19. who	why	when	where	who	whose
20. gets	got	goats	gets	goes	gems
21. ride	right	ready	ride	rode	rides
22. too	too	two	to	top	tow
23. we saw	we see	we saw	you say	you saw	we said
24. under	upper	until	understand	under	thunder
25. I will	I may	I want	I will	I won't	I wish

Exercise 7. Dolch: Primer

1. ate	eight	at	eat	ate	tea
2. no	on	no	one	now	won
3. you will	you were	you want	you win	you will	you were
4. want	went	want	twin	town	wall
5. where was	where were	were there	there were	where was	which was
6. all our	all our	all of	all hour	an hour	tall house
7. have it	have it	had it	has it	having it	half of it
8. but	bat	beet	bet	bit	but
9. so now	see now	sell now	send now	son now	so now
10. well	west	bell	tell	we'll	well
11. be	am	is	be	are	box
12. there	here	there	their	they're	it's here
13. he likes	she likes	it likes	he likes	we like	they like
14. white	white	went	while	which	whose
15. am	an	ask	am	me	us
16. into	in two	in this	into	upon	on my
17. came	came	come	comes	meat	cane
18. do you	did you do	do you	did you	have you	done for you
19. gets	get	get an	getting	bets	gets
20. yes, I am	yes, I'm	yes, I am	yes, we are	yes, I have	yes, I say
21. black	block	bland	black	below	blend
22. was not	is not	was for	is a note	wasn't a	was not
23. with me	with my	with you	with us	with me	with it
24. brown	brown	bread	throw	towel	trunk
25. say	said	stay	yes	say	sand

Exercise 8. Dolch: Primer

1. all our	all our	all your	all of	all in	allow
2. ran	run	ran	rain	real	ring
3. ride	rid	right	write	rode	ride
4. under the	under my	under a	under one	under this	under the
5. saw	was	saw	seen	scene	wasn't
6. eats	seat	easy	steam	eats	beats
7. will	wall	swell	well	will	while
8. with my	with me	with my	with us	with our	with you
9. but	boot	beat	bullet	tub	but
10. so	so	soon	to	do	go
11. ate two	tea two	eat two	ate two	at two	two mat
12. pretty	pretty	please	poor	purple	pretend
13. came	cane	canes	came	come	cube
14. for this	for them	for this	for that	for things	for these
15. do	done	did	does	do	dot
16. did she say	did he say	did they say	did she say	did one day	did she stay
17. be	be	bet	been	bean	do
18. are	were	or	are	ore	error
19. must	most	must	mist	more	money
20. with four	wish for	with friends	with four	with fools	with fun
21. ate	ate	at	tea	all	eat
22. now	know	no	new	row	now
23. wanted	wished	washed	watched	went	wanted
24. what is it	what it is	where is it	where she is	what is it	what it was
25. a good one	I took one	a good book	I won one	a good one	one good one

Exercise 9. Dolch: Primer

1. soon	son	sun	sunny	soon	so one
2. no	not	no	none	zero	to
3. we get	I get	you get	we get	they get	we're going
4. I saw a	he saw one	he saw a	I saw it	I saw a	I saw one
5. we have	we are	we need	we like	we have	we don't
6. there	here	these	those	they're	there
7. pretty	pretty	paid	purple	pushed	pulled
8. who do you	who do you	why do you	which do you	when do you	what do you
9. yes	yesterday	yeast	yes	yellow	yell
10. four	for	four	from	friend	first
11. please	plays	plans	please	prays	pretty
12. like	like	lake	luck	lick	lack
13. into	in two	in with	within	toward	into
14. rides	riding	writes	rails	lights	rides
15. they	them	then	they	these	those
16. he did	I did	he did	she did	they did	we did
17. black	blank	block	blend	brick	black
18. must	must	mist	mast	west	muddy
19. what is	what was	when is	what is	what was	while it's
20. too	ton	too	tune	took	tool
21. all the	all of	all they	all these	all the	all those
22. have	have	had	has	half	harm
23. that brown	that town	they drown	that frown	that black	that brown
24. good	goal	good	hood	book	heel
25. with	why	without	with us	with	within

Exercise 10. Dolch: Primer

1. good	good	book	look	took	hood
2. ride	read	ride	rides	rode	reads
3. please	pretty	plays	plans	please	plates
4. pretty	please	plates	witty	pretty	city
5. was	saw	went	were	has	was
6. and now	and new	are now	and know	are known	and now
7. like	look	lick	lack	like	lake
8. who saw	who was	how was	who saw	who said	who says
9. went	want	went	won't	window	wonder
10. so brown	so brown	so down	do black	so green	so strong
11. yes, we	yes, he	yes, she	yes, we	yes, they	yes, me
12. at the	in the	are the	at the	and then	and the
13. am now	am now	am not	are now	are not	ask now
14. into	onto	into	with	town	went
15. soon	son	sun	sooner	soon	some
16. eat	eats	seat	tea	ate	eat
17. on our	in our	at our	for our	our one	on our
18. must	mast	mist	most	must	moist
19. she	she	he	they	so	shell
20. he did	they did	she did	I did	we did	he did
21. this	these	this	those	that	them
22. what	what	who	how	where	when
23. four	from	four	found	fork	farm
24. good	gold	goal	good	mood	door
25. too	two	to	too	so	low

■ Exercise 11. Dolch: First Grade

1. could	cold	could	comb	hold	couldn't
2. takes	took	take	teak	takes	steak
3. living	living	leaving	bedding	eating	cooking
4. any in	many in	ant in	any in	candy in	army in
5. old	gold	bold	hold	old	told
6. going	going	getting	guessing	glowing	growing
7. give her	gave her	gave me	give her	give me	giving us
8. round	pound	mound	round	around	flown
9. thank you	thanks to you	think of you	thank you	thanking you	think about you
10. do again	did again	go again	be again	does again	do again
11. once	one	ones	once	twice	ounce
12. were	where	were	are	we're	we are
13. ask	talk	task	class	mask	ask
14. after	under	after	before	there	all of us
15. over	often	allow	other	over	oven
16. fly	free	fly	flake	try	cry
17. how did	how did	who did	when did	where did	why did
18. when is	when is	where is	hen is	who is	which is
19. open	a pen	opened	opener	pen on	open
20. for him	to him	for him	for his	to his	for he's
21. by	be	best	bee	by	fry
22. walk	work	walking	wreck	walk	we'll
23. from	falling	truck	friend	frame	from
24. think and	think and	wink and	these and	things and	three and
25. may	way	bay	more	mend	may

Exercise 12. Dolch: First Grade

1. an	am	arm	a.m.	aim	an
2. just	justice	yeast	yes	young	just
3. his	his	hits	hiss	him	is
4. as	as	ask	use	us	is
5. them	them	hems	hem	heat	these
6. of	if	on	of	up	for
7. had	hat	had	has	have	half
8. then	them	these	thin	then	they
9. let	tell	lit	let	lot	list
10. some of	same as	sunny in	send to	some of	come for
11. know	knife	know	knows	now	knew
12. stopped	stopping	stopped	stopper	topping	taped
13. put it in	put it on	put it at	but it is	put it in	but it has
14. once again	once more	once in	once again	once after	once for
15. walk	wake	walk	wakes	claw	walked
16. of	of	off	up	if	for
17. fly	flying	frying	follow	fly	fry
18. just them	just then	just this	just those	just these	just them
19. when did	when do	when does	when did	when days	when dirt
20. take	took	take	taking	taken	cake
21. every	very	evening	every	even	level
22. let him	let her	tell him	let them	let him	he let
23. she has	he has	she had	she was	he was	she has
24. them	them	then	these	those	hemmed
25. from me	for me	me first	from most	me then	from me

Exercise 13. Dolch: First Grade

1. over	cover	over	oven	mover	often
2. was how	was who	is how	is who	was how	who were
3. by	because	below	bought	been	by
4. give	gives	give	giving	gift	given
5. think	thank	thought	teeth	think	thing
6. for her	for here	for herself	for their	to hear	for her
7. open	oven	open	opened	opening	opens
8. his	his	him	hit	hiss	hill
9. thank you	thank you	think of you	thanks you	thing for you	thinks of you
10. were	we're	went	worry	we are	were
11. asking	assigning	talking	arranging	asking	aiming
12. of	on	of	in	if	out
13. any	any	money	many	none	candy
14. after	alter	awful	offend	after	and fat
15. put	pet	but	put	pot	part
16. and to live	and to live	and a life	and to leave	and living	and liver
17. know	knows	known	knowing	knowledge	know
18. may	marry	May	may	miss	mend
19. every	very	merry	every	delivery	recovery
20. had an	had an	have a	a hat	had a	half a
21. some know	some now	some knew	some know	some or	not some
22. as we walk	as we talk	as we call	as we want	as we work	as we walk
23. I could	I would	I should	I could	I called	I cough
24. then	them	then	these	their	things
25. round	really	around	found	round	ground

Exercise 14. Dolch: First Grade

1. just	jeans	just	guess	justice	yeast
2. asks	asks	asked	asking	tasks	masks
3. think of	thank you	think about	thinking	thought of	think of
4. may	may	May	miss	makes	map
5. could	cannot	could	couldn't	would	called
6. from you	from me	for you	from him	from you	for me
7. had it	has it	have it	eat it	had it	half of it
8. old	bold	cold	old	told	sold
9. after	until	allow	alter	before	after
10. only has	only has	only have	once has	only had	once have
11. put	pot	put	pat	pet	part
12. some	same	sane	some	soap	sum
13. how	how	who	has	hen	half
14. any	many	any	money	used	funny
15. every toy	each toy	all toys	every tall	every toy	very tall
16. over	ever	oven	other	over	cover
17. open them	open then	then open	over them	cover them	open them
18. by	be	but	buy	bye	by
19. as	has	add	at	as	ask
20. fly	fly	flies	flying	flew	flown
21. we often let	we often met	we often bet	we often let	we often tell	we often sit
22. lived	lives	living	live	alive	lived
23. walk	work	walk	wall	wake	walks
24. when do	when does	when did	when do	where do	where did
25. once	ones	ounce	once	only	one time

Exercise 15. Dolch: First Grade

1. takes	cakes	makes	takes	lakes	fakes
2. then	hen	thin	them	then	these
3. going now	doing now	being now	moving now	getting now	going now
4. giving	getting	giving	going	grinning	gaining
5. know	know	knows	knowledge	however	known
6. stop	tops	shop	stop	drops	pots
7. him and	hem and	him and	hen and	slim and	hit and
8. again	a gain	a game	age in	a goose	again
9. his	hits	him	hiss	his	he's
10. thank	thank	thanks	think	thinking	thinks
11. once	one's	ounce	once	only	one is
12. her	hear	heard	here	hour	her
13. but how	but who	but how	but why	but when	but he's
14. may know	may know	may see	may grow	may take	may show
15. could do	could go	could be	could if	could do	could move
16. give	give	gift	fight	live	gave
17. think	thank	thanks	think	thinking	thinks
18. from	frame	frozen	friend	from	freeze
19. old	cold	hold	told	fold	old
20. going	goes	gone	going	gold	giving
21. just her	just hear	just here	just him	just her	just heard
22. to fly	to free	to fly	to fry	to try	to my friend
23. asking for	asked for	asking for	making for	calling for	aiming for
24. any	many	city	lively	any	pretty
25. puts	pots	pays	step	pets	puts

Exercise 16. Dolch: Second Grade

1. cold	called	could	cold	can't	gold
2. sleep	slip	slept	sweep	keep	sleep
3. very	every	even	berry	very	bury
4. many	any	money	many	mostly	man
5. because	below the	be the cause	be a cause	be a friend	because
6. she tells	she's tall	she tells	he's tall	he tells	she told
7. right	right	write	light	reach	roach
8. I don't	I didn't	I don't	I do not	I couldn't	I can't
9. fast	fails	feast	first	fist	fast
10. before now	be for now	because now	be near now	before now	be low now
11. found	ground	round	found	blond	friend
12. why	why	when	which	way	worry
13. they would	they worry	they would	they could	they wished	they walked
14. off	of	cuff	oven	off	laugh
15. its	it is	it's	is it	hits	its
16. five or	five of	five in	five or	fire or	fist on
17. always	awful	all the way	angry	artist	always
18. first	fist	first	fast	fourth	fears
19. use one	use one	using one	use once	useful once	used one
20. been	been	bone	ban	bean	beef
21. and both	and both	and a bath	and bought	and a bottle	and post
22. best	vest	bath	both	bees	best
23. I work	I walk	I wish	I want	I work	I will
24. call	cold	could	call	called	I'll
25. goes	ghost	going	does	goes	golf

■ *Exercise 17. Dolch: Second Grade*

1. or green	or grown	or green	or grind	or grain	or groan
2. pull	bull	pulled	pill	pull	pills
3. read	ready	dear	road	write	read
4. they buy	they buy	they try	they cry	they pray	they beg
5. write	right	tire	write	wired	wire
6. their	them	there	they're	their	these
7. upon	up	on	only	upon	uncle
8. does	does	did	doing	toes	dust
9. sit	sat	set	soot	seat	sit
10. sing	song	sang	sung	sin	sing
11. wash	wish	wash	work	worst	was
12. made	make	mad	male	made	mad
13. always	awful	always	all of a	a way	many ways
14. us	is	as	us	use	ice
15. of these	of these	of the sea	of the seats	of things	of those
16. which	which	where	when	whenever	whose
17. now your	now you're	now your	now you are	now you	now you and
18. around	round	ground	around	astound	a round
19. if you wish	if you wash	if you mash	if your wish	if you fish	if you wish
20. pulls	pulled	pulling	bulls	pulls	balls
21. cold then	gold then	called then	cold then	cloud then	clock then
22. write	write	writes	read	rights	reads
23. we don't	we didn't	he doesn't	we do not	he does not	we don't
24. I sleep	I slip	I slap	I sleep	I am slow	I shop
25. very	every	event	even	valley	very

Exercise 18. Dolch: Second Grade

1. five of	file of	fire in	fight at	favor of	five of
2. those	hose	thorns	those	these	there's
3. wash	wish	wash	mash	most	show
4. their green	their grand	their great	this green	their green	those green
5. first	first	fast	fist	for sale	fits
6. sit here	sat here	fit here	this here	sit here	site here
7. their	they're	these	there	their	the air
8. many use	most use	money use	many use	must use	may use
9. off	of	off	if	up	cuff
10. we sleep	we sleep	we slept	we spell	we peel	we spill
11. upon	up in	upper	upon	pond	spoon
12. buy or	buy it	buy off	buy one	buy or	buy only
13. or it would	or it would	or it won't	or it's wood	or it could	or it's worse
14. tell us	tells us	told us	talk to us	take us	tell us
15. cold	gold	old	cold	bold	called
16. always	awful	always	and then	all waste	all right
17. before	busy	buy for	be for	restore	before
18. don't tell	don't take	don't sell	don't tell	don't touch	don't teach
19. around	found	round	astound	ground	around
20. call this	kill this	call these	cold this	call this	kill these
21. because	become	because	be careful	be near	be a cause
22. sing	song	sing	sang	sung	singer
23. why	why	which	where	when	who
24. tell	tall	till	let	least	tell
25. made	made	make	makes	making	male

Exercise 19. Dolch: Second Grade

1. found	fixed	found	fired	friend	field
2. its	it's	is	isn't	its	sit
3. because	beware	because	beginning	below	better
4. gave	gave	given	giver	have	give
5. always	almost	always	awful	angry	allow
6. or right	or reach	or right	or roast	or rooster	or light
7. does your	do you	did your	did you	does just	does your
8. these	things	those	them	thoughts	these
9. before you	because you	below you	be for you	before you	follow you
10. very cold	very old	very bold	every cold	very cold	your hold
11. which	witch	which	where	whenever	white
12. five green	five green	give green	first, go	five grain	from grain
13. been	bean	being	bone	teen	been
14. or	on	of	or	nor	old
15. like us	lake use	like ours	like me	like us	like this
16. buy	buy	burn	been	bug	book
17. called	could	calling	cold	canceled	called
18. goes	going	does	goes	moves	golden
19. best	bear	vest	test	best	dentist
20. which was	which was	when was	whose was	where was	weather was
21. off	off	of	if	on	only
22. use	us	fuse	house	using	use
23. those	this	these	those	hose	closet
24. and would	and could	and worry	and would	and wonder	and will
25. fast	fist	first	fast	waste	cast

Exercise 20. Dolch: Second Grade

1. wish	wash	wish	show	fish	wrench
2. first	fist	fast	frost	first	second
3. sit	sat	sit	set	soot	it's
4. both	bottom	bother	both	broth	brother
5. many	money	any	man	mainly	many
6. made	mad	dam	made	mole	male
7. green	grain	groan	ground	green	grass
8. around	allowed	aprons	around	round	ground
9. working	walking	worrying	worth	worked	working
10. read	ready	reads	reader	read	redden
11. wash	wash	wish	show	fish	worse
12. use these	use this	use them	use these	used these	used this
13. and very	and very	and every	and even	and easy	and early
14. found one	found on	find on	find one	found one	finally it
15. fast	fast	first	fist	feast	frost
16. sing	songs	sang	singer	sings	sing
17. these	these	this	those	things	there's
18. your best	you're best	your west	your vest	you're very	your best
19. first, you	fast, you	first, you	fist, you	feast, you	frost, you
20. which	where	wishes	whenever	while	which
21. goes very	goes every	goes very	glows very	does every	does very
22. read your	reads you	reads your	read your	reading you	read you
23. sleep	sleep	slept	keep	bleed	bleeds
24. call us	call as	call us	call is	call off	call for
25. those	clothes	dozen	these	those	there's

Exercise 21. Dolch: Third Grade

1. show	worse	whose	show	shows	who is
2. laugh	laugh	laughs	lasted	lounge	lunches
3. drink	drank	drunk	dark	think	drink
4. eight	eaten	eight	eating	early	eerie
5. myself	myself	my safe	my silk	my sofa	my sand
6. was small	is small	as small	were small	was small	does small
7. ten of	often	of tin	ton of	then of	ten of
8. if only	if one	one if	optional	if only	only if
9. got	get	gets	got	gotten	gadget
10. and it grows	and it throws	and it grows	and it flows	and it goes	and it snows
11. never	nearer	never	every	ever	neither
12. together	to gather	to get her	tomorrow	toward	together
13. fall if	fell if	fallen if	fold if	fill if	fall if
14. light	later	light	right	lastly	fight
15. keep up	keep in	keep off	keep up	keep at	keep near
16. done	doing	clown	done	tone	down
17. hurt	hard	heart	hurt	turned	hurl
18. hold	held	hold	cold	bold	told
19. clean up	clean up	cleans up	cleaned up	clean off	cleaned off
20. carry	carries	curry	marry	carry	worry
21. much	much	many	must	most	mist
22. isn't far	isn't farther	isn't for	isn't fear	isn't fair	isn't far
23. today	this day	too late	to Monday	today	tomorrow
24. small	small	smell	smile	skull	snail
25. keep	feet	deep	feed	keep	steep

Exercise 22. Dolch: Third Grade

1. long	lawn	last	short	lean	long
2. own six	own two	own one	own six	own tax	on six
3. about	above	about	abroad	abrupt	apron
4. draw	draw	straw	drew	threw	thaw
5. hot	hot	got	lot	not	pot
6. ten of	ten in	often	ten off	ten of	ten up
7. full	fall	fill	feel	full	felt
8. growing	growing	blowing	showing	knowing	throwing
9. never far	never for	ever far	never far	ever for	even far
10. bring	spring	bring	thing	think	drink
11. kind of	kind of	kind is	kind are	kind from	kind for
12. starts with	part with	parts with	start with	starts with	start to wish
13. warm	warn	ward	harm	worm	warm
14. not to try	not to fry	not to cry	not to fly	not to try	not to dry
15. drink	spring	bring	thing	drink	think
16. done	down	done	dust	drown	tone
17. only ten	ten of	ten only	often	from ten	only ten
18. hold	hello	held	hold	home	holy
19. carry	clean	marry	very	every	carry
20. if	it	is	if	off	of
21. better	best	bottle	better	bitter	batter
22. pick	pack	pick	piece	pickle	packages
23. got by the	got to buy	got but then	got by them	got to the	got by the
24. cut	cut	cute	cuts	but	got
25. today	tonight	today	daylight	days	toddler

Exercise 23. Dolch: Third Grade

1. own	now	own	know	won	woman
2. today	tonight	this day	to date	today	toddler
3. carry then	carry them	carry then	marry then	marry them	worry then
4. better	bitter	bottle	butter	batter	better
5. warn us	warm us	warn you	worms and	warn us	wars but
6. try	try	fry	cry	sly	dry
7. draw	draw	flower	drew	flaw	drawer
8. done	doing	down	done	deed	bone
9. have ten	have then	then have	ten have	have ten	often
10. together	gathering	to get her	together	to gather	tackle
11. hot in the	hit in the	hat in the	hot in the	not in the	got in the
12. light	right	tight	sight	might	light
13. if they	if there	if these	if they	if those	if this
14. pick	pick	choose	press	clock	first
15. cut	cute	cutter	cutting	cuts	cut
16. fall	fail	fall	foul	file	fell
17. show	how's	snow	shower	shown	show
18. laughing so	laughing to	laughing, so	landing, so	laughing so	landing so
19. hold	hold	hiked	boiled	hole	bold
20. and it got	and a cot	and a copy	and it let	and it had	and it got
21. clean	claim	clear	clean	brain	bleed
22. full	full	fill	fall	follow	feel
23. much	must	much	many	mash	muddy
24. hurt	heart	harmed	hurl	hurt	hold
25. only these	once these	only these	lonely these	alone these	one of these

Exercise 24. Dolch: Third Grade

1. long	lone	long	allowed	loud	lost
2. was drinking	was dreaming	was blinking	was thinking	was winking	was drinking
3. clean	clear	lean	beans	cleared	clean
4. about	above	allowed	around	alive	about
5. six	six	sex	socks	seems	tax
6. done	down	done	need one	do one	drown
7. and draw	and draw	and drew	and thaw	and straw	and flaw
8. myself	myself	me and	my safe	my sent	my selfish
9. fall	fail	fallen	feel	fall	fell
10. only	once	lonely	only	alone	one
11. eight	seven	nine	three	eight	four
12. it brings	it rings	it brings	it drinks	it borrows	it sings
13. carry	carry	marry	ferry	every	worry
14. keep	kept	keys	peak	peek	keep
15. better now	bitter now	butter now	better now	batter now	bother now
16. grow too	grew too	grow to	grew to	grow too	grows to
17. seven	even	seven	saved	stolen	several
18. warm	swarm	army	worm	warm	worth
19. very kind	every kind	every kid	very kind	several kids	every knife
20. much	most	many	such	much	touch
21. they never	they noted	they neared	they nailed	they needed	they never
22. hurt	heart	hurt	harmed	Thursday	here
23. started them	start them	starting them	started them	to start them	starts them
24. far	far	fear	fan	for	fur
25. light	tight	flight	light	right	sight

Exercise 25. Dolch: Third Grade

1. your drink	you drink	you drank	your drinks	your ring	your drink
2. shows	shown	showers	shows	showing	showed
3. seven	seventy	several	seven	saved	saving
4. fall	fell	filled	full	follow	fall
5. far	for	fear	fan	far	fur
6. kind of	kind to	kind for	kind of	kind with	kind in
7. laugh	laughter	laugh	laughing	laughed	laughs
8. today	today	Monday	Friday	Tuesday	Thursday
9. start with	starts with	starts to	start when	start with	start to
10. hold	holding	holds	hold	held	whole
11. small	smile	malls	mills	stall	small
12. full	fell	full	filled	follow	fall
13. eight	five	six	seven	eight	nine
14. she tries	she dries	she tries	she buys	she cries	she plays
15. long	long	longer	longest	lonely	lower
16. never	never	nicest	nearest	newest	nodded
17. your cuts	your cats	your cat	your cuts	your cut	you're cut
18. hot	hot	hit	hat	heat	hurt
19. own	own	owl	owner	owns	owning
20. about	above	around	allow	about	abrupt
21. they pick	the pig	the pill	they pack	they put	they pick
22. bring	ring	bring	swing	drink	thing
23. if only	if one	if they	if we	if alone	if only
24. isn't today	isn't Tuesday	isn't tonight	isn't for today	isn't today	isn't tomorrow
25. seven	several	seven	eleven	seventeen	success

Exercise 26. Beginning

1. if they are	in them are	of them are	if they are	it is their	is the art
2. piece	point	people	pieces	points	piece
3. movie	movies	move	movie	more	maybe
4. have one	have one	had one	has one	haven't one	hasn't one
5. once	one	only	other	old	once
6. young	your	you're	year	young	just
7. and bird	and birds	and book	and book	and bird	and beard
8. deal	deal	deaf	feel	food	dead
9. below	begin	below	began	brown	blow
10. start	state	states	star	stars	start
11. this year	this year	these years	this young	this good	this fear
12. is	it's	is	in	of	if
13. last	late	last	letter	list	lost
14. Georgia is	Germany is	Orange is	Cleopatra is	George is	Georgia is
15. wanted	wants	wanted	worried	worries	want
16. made	many	made	mad	makes	make
17. lines	likes	lives	lines	limes	lights
18. from	form	for	four	from	foot
19. partner	parent	people	partner	between	parts
20. was in	was in	well in	wasn't in	wash in	watch in
21. smoke	small	short	shoes	smoke	secret
22. grew and	grow and	group and	good and	year and	grew and
23. many	many	more	most	much	man
24. different	difficult	discusses	describe	different	differ
25. take an	half an	have an	take an	make an	lake an

Exercise 27. Beginning

1. that	this	then	they	that	hats
2. Florida	Florence	Florida	France	Finland	French
3. found	from	found	find	finds	forward
4. ideas	ideas	deals	taste	idea	ice
5. the people	the people	the piece	the points	the pieces	the point
6. write	writes	wrote	winter	write	writing
7. his	her	he's	him	has	his
8. a famous	a farmer	a famous	a family	a fatter	a father
9. your	you	young	your	year	yellow
10. one small	sell one	one snail	one smell	one small	one smile
11. first	frying	fist	first	firm	fills
12. wasn't very	wasn't very	weren't very	isn't very	aren't very	won't vary
13. this	these	they	that	those	this
14. it's	he's	isn't	it's	she's	we're
15. read	dear	red	dead	aren't	read
16. about	able	about	around	allow	aloud
17. really thick	really think	really thinks	really thick	really thirsty	really thirty
18. also	also	other	shoe	elbow	into
19. there	their	they've	there	here	where
20. thought none	thought none	thought more	thought nose	thought moon	thought noon
21. choice	choices	chooses	cheese	choice	choose
22. writer	wrote	writing	writes	wrong	writer
23. then thirteen	then fourteen	then thirty	then forty	then thirteen	then thirsty
24. saw Douglas	saw Donald	saw Dennis	saw Daniel	saw David	saw Douglas
25. author	artist	author	answer	allowing	operator

Exercise 28. Beginning

1. this helps	this helps	this helped	this help	this hopes	this hoped
2. two	too	out	two	tea	toe
3. died	lied	died	dead	feed	tied
4. and he played	and he plays	and he's playing	and he played	and a player	and we played
5. flamingo	flames	flamingos	farmers	flamingo	mango
6. isn't	don't	aren't	wasn't	it's	isn't
7. happen	happen	pepper	paper	happy	happened
8. easy quiz	easy test	easy guess	easy quiz	easy question	easy task
9. tell	tells	tall	tell	till	toll
10. only then	once then	lonely then	alone then	one then	only then
11. correct	collect	correct	corner	corners	collects
12. talk	fork	talk	talks	forks	talked
13. she'll	they'll	he'll	we'll	you'll	she'll
14. smoker	smoked	smoking	smokes	smoke	smoker
15. why	who	when	where	why	what
16. also	also	into	under	always	all's
17. a big day	a big dog	a big dam	a big day	a big play	a big toy
18. great	greet	great	ground	grilled	grand
19. Florida	Florida	France	French	Finland	Florence
20. where were	when were	when are	where are	where were	what were
21. famous	famous	farmers	fathers	feathers	families
22. out	our	own	cut	out	off
23. in circles	in a circle	in color	in a circus	in colors	in circles
24. for	four	for	form	far	fur
25. five or	fire or	file or	fine or	five or	fold or

Exercise 29. Beginning

1. they took	they take	they took	they cook	they look	their hook
2. but	bat	boat	bit	but	nut
3. month	money	mouth	month	north	south
4. or the office	or the offer	or the office	of they're off	or the official	of their office
5. out	off	our	out	eat	old
6. rule	rail	lost	runs	role	rule
7. difficult	difficult	different	differed	discuss	discussed
8. between us	between us	below us	behind us	between its	better beans
9. wrong	wrong	among	write	wrote	wrapped
10. groups	grapes	group	grape	groups	ground
11. then	them	this	these	that	then
12. off	on	our	own	of	off
13. tree to	true to	towel to	time to	tree to	free to
14. house	horse	house	how's	horses	houses
15. actor	actress	acted	actor	artist	acting
16. each	ache	every	peach	teach	each
17. well now	wall now	will now	well now	tell now	bell now
18. really tired	really tired	really tried	really tries	really tires	really tied
19. age	ate	age	ache	egg	page
20. born	burn	born	burned	barn	barns
21. and main	and main	and mail	and made	and map	and pain
22. really	real	redder	rainy	really	rainy
23. helped	helping	helper	helps	help	helped
24. organ is	only is	organs is	oddest is	organ is	once is
25. people	person	persons	people	piece	pieces

Exercise 30. Beginning

1. those days	those stays	those dogs	those days	those dolls	those don't
2. cloth	clean	clear	clothing	cloth	clown
3. it	if	it	is	at	of
4. walking	walked	worked	walks	working	walking
5. however	houses	however	whenever	whoever	forever
6. happens	happy	happen	happens	happened	happier
7. crane	crab	cane	rain	crane	cranes
8. folk	yolk	four	folk	fork	talk
9. did	did	didn't	do	doesn't	dad
10. only said	only salt	only sad	only says	only sand	only said
11. if	if	of	us	off	it
12. and now he's	and now she's	and now it's	and now he's	and now his	and now her
13. have	has	had	hats	have	haven't
14. small, but	smile, but	smell, but	shell, but	small, but	malls, but
15. found	found	finds	finding	ground	find
16. not	note	not	nut	notes	ton
17. coworker	coteacher	worker	coworker	teacher	coworkers
18. book with	book wish	book with	book want	book wishes	book water
19. should tie	should lie	should tie	shouldn't tie	shouldn't lie	should die
20. things	thinks	think	thirsty	things	thing
21. get	get	got	gas	gold	jet
22. later	late	fatter	latest	laser	later
23. the queen	the queens	the quick	the green	the quiet	the queen
24. make	made	making	Mike	male	make
25. said again	said again	sad again	same again	salt again	sold again

■ *Exercise 31. Beginning*

1. about	always	also	above	agree	about
2. blue in	blue in	blood in	black in	glue in	true in
3. either	eastern	neither	either	feather	faster
4. city	cities	city	stay	silly	cool
5. first, you	fast, you	faster, you	fist, you	feast, you	first, you
6. John	Jack	June	Jane	John	jump
7. liked	likes	like	alike	liked	linked
8. public	puddle	public	bubble	poodle	under
9. the team	the time	the team	the meat	the tame	the steam
10. these	these	those	that's	there	them
11. author	artist	article	although	authors	author
12. child	child	hill	chill	hide	China
13. buy	buys	bought	boys	boy	buy
14. very difficult	very different	every different	very difficult	every disease	every different
15. more	move	some	Rome	most	more
16. name	mean	main	name	names	named
17. used	uses	used	using	user	use
18. they were	them were	they were	stay were	days were	hay were
19. ended	ended	ending	ends	endings	sender
20. rare	real	rare	are	roar	room
21. and that small	and that smell	and that small	and that smile	and that mall	and that mile
22. idea	ideas	area	areas	idle	idea
23. however	whenever	whoever	however	wherever	whether
24. your books	your books	your book	your banks	your bank	your boots
25. after that	always that	also that	after that	feather that	afraid that

Exercise 32. Beginning

1. and then died	and then dead	and then died	and then deal	and then diet	and then tied
2. colors	color	coming	colors	collars	collar
3. said	sand	said	says	saying	sail
4. a flock	a flood	a film	a flag	a clock	a flock
5. start	stars	star	starts	started	start
6. I wrote	I write	I wrap	I rode	I wrote	I would
7. every	ever	very	every	even	event
8. but	but	ban	bump	put	pun
9. area	are	real	rear	arena	area
10. age	age	ago	ice	ore	old
11. the best game	the best games	the best game	the best names	the best name	the best gum
12. other	others	allow	bother	other	oven
13. penguin	purpose	pencil	penguin	penguins	purposes
14. could	couldn't	would	should	could	wouldn't
15. to move	to model	to most	to move	to moan	to store
16. free if	flee if	tree if	fried if	fresh if	free if
17. protect	publish	public	protect	protects	publishes
18. young	younger	young	year	years	yours
19. one disease	one different	one difficult	one disaster	one disease	one death
20. June	June	John	Jean	July	Joan
21. by	be	to	at	my	by
22. any	many	ant	any	only	icy
23. famous for	feet for	find for	feather for	farmers for	famous for
24. wings	wing	wind	wings	swing	wigs
25. time	tips	team	timer	times	time

Exercise 33. Beginning

1. box	box	boxes	but	buy	buys
2. join in	jeans in	join in	coin in	coins in	joke in
3. people	person	purple	people	played	parent
4. stars	start	starts	rats	stars	star
5. world	would	wind	word	words	world
6. a king	a kind	a gift	a fight	a knife	a king
7. began	begin	become	behind	began	begun
8. flag	flat	flap	flag	glad	flow
9. were others	were always	were other	were others	were ones	was another
10. some	same	some	come	game	gone
11. the states	the states	the state	the stays	the stay	the steaks
12. very bad	every bad	even bad	every bid	every bed	very bad
13. for	four	for	fur	far	her
14. air	hair	ear	air	aid	aim
15. however	whoever	however	whenever	everyone	wherever
16. either	eastern	teacher	neither	painter	either
17. read to	road to	reads to	roads to	read to	reach to
18. finds	find	finds	minds	mind	winds
19. is	it	as	us	is	it's
20. the person	the people	the person	the purple	the purpose	the purposes
21. could	could	couldn't	would	wouldn't	called
22. children	child	brothers	parents	children	sister
23. but	bat	bet	bit	buy	but
24. money	many	monkey	money	monkeys	marry
25. she likes	she likes	she liked	she lights	she lives	she lies

Exercise 34. Beginning

1. he wrote	we wrote	he wrote	she wrote	he writes	she writes
2. use	used	use	uses	fuse	music
3. well	wall	will	when	wetter	well
4. model	money	many	modern	model	made
5. the eggs	the eggs	the egg	the legs	the leg	they sell
6. died	dies	tied	dead	die	died
7. career	carry	career	common	cancer	called
8. by today	be today	by today	boy today	buy today	my birthday
9. all	call	ill	all	art	old
10. just in	just on	just in	just an	just is	just if
11. stripe	strip	trip	trips	strips	stripe
12. red	red	dear	read	bed	wed
13. best parents	best people	best parent	best person	best purpose	best parents
14. only	once	only	alone	lonely	one
15. none	noisy	know	none	some	nose
16. most	most	storm	mist	must	mast
17. lived	lives	living	liver	loved	lived
18. was their	wash their	saw their	was their	worst there	west then
19. write	written	wrote	writing	writes	write
20. very early	even ears	even earth	very early	very eastern	very curly
21. could	couldn't	can't	pound	called	could
22. about	apron	about	bother	another	among
23. reply	really	reply	replied	repay	response
24. slow	lower	slow	slower	slowest	low
25. and they	and them	and this	and they	and they're	and these

Exercise 35. Beginning

1. about	after	although	anyone	artist	about
2. this job for	this job form	this job far	this job for	this job from	this job first
3. case	care	case	cares	cases	cures
4. stolen	steal	stronger	spoken	token	stolen
5. some art	some art	some tar	some rats	some are	some ears
6. died	dead	dies	tied	died	fried
7. large groups	large group	large ground	large groups	large green	large grains
8. liked	likes	liked	looks	looked	lucky
9. plays	played	tray	trays	play	plays
10. isn't rare	isn't rare	isn't ready	isn't real	isn't meat	isn't near
11. books	books	book	good	hooks	hook
12. home	time	home	house	honest	phone
13. every	every	very	everyone	everything	earth
14. with	wish	with	west	wind	white
15. these stripes	these trips	these strips	this trip	this stripe	these stripes
16. she isn't	he's not	she's not	it isn't	she isn't	he isn't
17. flag	flow	flag	flows	flags	flying
18. career	careers	cancer	career	callers	caller
19. I call	I called	I call	I'm cold	I've called	I'm calling
20. author	artist	author	authors	artists	earlier
21. model	modern	money	model	label	noodle
22. young	yearly	younger	youngest	yesterday	young
23. very nicely	very nicely	every nicely	vary nicely	weary now	early now
24. eggs	legs	begs	goes	egg	eggs
25. born	barn	burn	brown	town	born

Exercise 36. Beginning

1. day	days	say	hay	day	says
2. our boat	our boats	our boots	our bowl	our boat	our boot
3. built	build	built	beetle	belts	building
4. area	are	arid	area	hair	ears
5. captain	capital	captain	capitals	captains	carpet
6. hole	older	hold	hole	heel	hold
7. four elevators	four electric	four elevator	four enormous	four elevators	four examples
8. icy and	ice and	ace and	easy and	lazy and	icy and
9. first, they	fast, they	fist, they	furs, they	burst, they	first, they
10. he donated	he donates	she donates	he donated	he's donating	he's a donor
11. enough	every	exact	example	enormous	enough
12. has	had	have	he's	his	has
13. deaf	leaf	head	deaf	deal	dead
14. than	then	that	this	than	thin
15. states	statue	states	started	start	statues
16. or leave	or large	or leaves	or left	or leave	or larger
17. miles	mine	males	smile	miles	mile
18. married	marry	married	worried	worries	hurried
19. invention	inventor	invented	inventions	invent	invention
20. smaller	smallest	small	smiled	smaller	speller
21. one	only	once	one	tone	bone
22. site	sit	sat	bite	site	sitting
23. to sink	to sink	to sin	to see	to think	to sing
24. ranks	rang	rings	ranked	rank	ranks
25. the oldest	the old	the older	the coldest	the boldest	the oldest

Exercise 37. Beginning

1. later	late	later	latest	letter	lettuce
2. island	island	answer	information	isn't	aisle
3. nearby	nothing	nearer	nearest	newest	nearby
4. looks	lost	look	books	desks	looks
5. and nine	and mine	and nine	and line	and name	and mean
6. long	lose	lone	alone	long	longer
7. named	names	named	name	meaning	mended
8. millions	million	miller	millers	millions	hundreds
9. money	months	monkey	money	monkeys	month
10. saw tons	saw stone	saw stones	saw tones	saw tons	saw sons
11. squares	stairs	squeals	squares	square	statues
12. me their	me there	me these	me they're	me their	me these
13. died	dead	head	deaf	deal	died
14. were very	were very	we're very	went very	very wet	very weary
15. this deer	that deer	these deer	his deer	this deer	those deer
16. worked	working	works	worked	worker	wasted
17. man	men	man	many	name	mean
18. world	would	worlds	worry	world	worried
19. such	sick	much	sack	touch	such
20. the time	the times	the time	the dime	the dimes	the lime
21. year	rear	young	year	years	younger
22. are students	are studies	are students	are stories	are stamps	are stores
23. visitor	visited	visiting	visitor	vastly	monitor
24. tuna	unit	tuna	nuts	tuba	nuts
25. your tip	your top	your tab	your tip	your type	your dip

Exercise 38. Beginning

1. sink them	sing them	think then	sink then	sing then	sink them
2. three	tree	three	trees	trays	threes
3. soup	soup	soap	sour	sound	seed
4. heart	heard	heart	head	heat	hear
5. a capital	a captain	a capital	a carpet	a chapter	a cap of
6. main	mean	mine	main	mind	mean
7. cover	could	cover	over	covered	couldn't
8. came	came	cane	come	camel	name
9. group	groups	green	grab	group	greatly
10. miles	meals	mills	miles	mile	smiles
11. of them went	of them went	of them were	of them want	of them are	of them was
12. part	port	parts	ports	part	pardon
13. sign on	sign on	signs on	sigh on	sighs on	sight on
14. deals	leads	deal	lead	deals	able
15. chips	chip	chop	cheap	chips	chops
16. saw a barber	saw a baker	was a barber	saw a barber	was a bakery	was a beeper
17. there now	there now	these now	things now	those now	them now
18. offices	offers	offer	office	after	offices
19. women	woman	women	warmer	worms	wisdom
20. ate the salad	eat the salty	eat the salad	ate the soup	ate the salty	ate the salad
21. inside	internal	outside	inside	insight	island
22. world's	wouldn't	worlds	wheels	world's	shouldn't
23. Canadian	Canada	Colombian	Canadian	Colombia	Cairo
24. in France	in French	at Fran's	in Finland	to France	in France
25. concrete	concrete	conceal	conceit	covered	construction

Exercise 39. Beginning

1. as gold	as good	as cold	has gold	has old	as gold
2. some farms	some forms	same frame	same farm	some frames	some farms
3. people	person	people	purple	present	papers
4. mine	mind	many	mine	main	mean
5. now fish	new fish	now fresh	now fish	new fence	new dish
6. times	time	times	dime	dimes	timed
7. every	ever	never	everyone	everything	every
8. many daily	many deals	many dusty	many deadly	many daily	many deaths
9. first, our	fresh, our	fist, our	thirst, our	worst, our	first, our
10. Boston	Baldwin	Britain	Boston	Bartholdi	Black
11. companies	continuous	construction	colonies	companies	chemicals
12. health	health	heart	steal	wealth	teeth
13. came in a	came in a	come in a	name in a	same in a	cane in a
14. a boy could	a boy called	a boy's coats	a boy would	a boy should	a boy could
15. big	box	beg	big	bag	bit
16. a good base	a good face	a good hose	a good base	a good vase	a good voice
17. about	above	about	aboard	abduct	abundant
18. faces	face	faced	faces	favorite	faucet
19. rude	door	ready	running	rude	crude
20. soup	soap	stoop	stop	soup	sour
21. this high	this huge	this height	this sigh	this high	this laugh
22. inside	outside	insider	outsider	inside	inward
23. family	famous	family	families	framed	fancy
24. as	is	us	it	at	as
25. from now	from now	form now	forms now	harm now	farm now

Exercise 40. Beginning

1. is cheese	was cheese	is cheese	was cream	is cream	is cheap
2. all tips	all pits	all tips	small tips	small pits	all tops
3. tuna	nuts	ton	stone	tune	tuna
4. a big base	a big case	a big nose	a big bay	a big box	a big base
5. born	born	brain	torn	four	form
6. wood	weed	good	hood	wood	would
7. every cut	every cat	every cot	every cut	every cute	every cup
8. axe	oxen	box	tax	axe	ice
9. silver	servant	silver	seven	served	slipper
10. pointed	painted	points	paints	pointed	printed
11. gold	cold	sold	bold	mold	gold
12. loudly	loudly	cloudy	proudly	boldly	carefully
13. they chop	they shop	they hop	they're cheap	they hope	they chop
14. afraid	after	affirm	arid	afraid	fried
15. wind	wind	wand	went	winter	windy
16. hands	hand	stands	lands	hands	land
17. baby cried	baby tried	baby cried	baby cry	baby tries	baby cries
18. trees	three	thirst	tears	trees	tree
19. down	town	down	gown	dawn	damp
20. began	began	begin	begun	bring	shrank
21. ghost	gross	green	guest	ghosts	ghost
22. about two	above two	about to	about two	abroad to	after two
23. chose	chose	shoes	choose	chosen	chore
24. poor	pear	pair	door	boot	poor
25. forest with	friends with	forest with	forests with	friend with	fourth wish

Exercise 41. Intermediate

1.	think	thin	thing	think	this	thinks
2.	when	where	hen	when	which	wet
3.	or bought	or brought	or ought	or taught	or buys	or bought
4.	sing	skiing	sink	sane	sing	sings
5.	couldn't eat	couldn't sit	couldn't take	can't eat	couldn't eat	can't take
6.	take	take	lake	rake	make	ache
7.	to fasten	to listen	to fatten	to fasten	to hasten	to fast
8.	mean	main	name	nail	mean	mane
9.	rear	ear	rare	roar	oar	rear
10.	say that	sea that	says that	stay that	say that	bay that
11.	pies	pea	pie	spy	spies	pies
12.	fear	fear	feet	feel	ear	far
13.	the tent	the ten	the next	the tents	the tent	the net
14.	sea	see	sea	ease	ear	say
15.	your rings	your rings	your ring	you sing	your risk	you sink
16.	kiss	skin	kills	kill	kiss	skill
17.	with	thin	with	this	which	what
18.	soup	soups	spoon	soap	soar	soup
19.	ask	asks	tax	ask	has	ax
20.	if it had	if they have	if it had	if it's at	if it	if his
21.	thin	chin	shin	chop	thin	this
22.	four	four	for	fear	fort	foul
23.	and do	and did	and be	and so	and you	and do
24.	coal	cool	coat	cold	comb	coal
25.	hats	has	haste	at	hats	heat

Exercise 42. Intermediate

1. an act	a tax	an ace	enact	an act	a tack
2. time	site	times	lime	limes	time
3. day	dog	yard	days	did	day
4. your key	your key	your keys	you keep	your kite	your kit
5. ten	tan	ton	ten	tin	tea
6. stay	sap	says	stay	stays	yes
7. curve	carve	race	curve	carves	curves
8. very fine	every fish	find every	every fin	very fit	very fine
9. prints	paint	paints	prints	print	points
10. does	time	dime	does	tea	dead
11. shall not	no shell	shall not	no halls	no hills	should not
12. when you	went to	where does	whom you	wish you	when you
13. eyes	easy	yes	eyes	eye	says
14. copy with	coffee with	stop with	loving with	copies with	copy with
15. for	four	fat	food	for	fear
16. might	must	should	night	could	might
17. hear	hear	ear	near	ears	high
18. this pen	this pen	this pan	this pin	these pens	they spent
19. main	aims	name	man	mean	main
20. it's	its	is	it's	sit	isn't
21. has to pick	has to peek	has to peak	has to pack	has to pick	had to pick
22. read	read	rear	dear	red	reads
23. near	ear	neat	rear	near	need
24. put	put	pot	pet	pit	pat
25. does	dead	did	don't	does	goes

Exercise 43. Intermediate

1.	cow	how	low	cow	row	now
2.	lamp	land	palm	lamps	plant	lamp
3.	and here	am here	an ear	hand here	and here	ate here
4.	fly	fly	flies	flew	fill	full
5.	are	read	and	rear	art	are
6.	cup	caps	cups	cap	cup	cop
7.	the bed	the beds	the bad	the bed	the body	the bet
8.	card	car	cart	cat	card	care
9.	burst	trust	brush	burst	beast	bursts
10.	over there	over three	over these	over there	over this	over the
11.	then	these	them	there	then	they
12.	send	tent	sell	sends	sells	send
13.	mop	map	mop	maps	mops	mud
14.	is a pen	is a pan	is a pen	is a pin	is a pie	is a pea
15.	be	am	do	by	is	be
16.	at ten	am ten	at ten	all ten	are ten	an end
17.	reads it	read it	need it	needs it	reads it	reading it
18.	keep	key	keep	keeps	keys	keeping
19.	chicken	cheap	kitchen	children	cheese	chicken
20.	see sheep	see shoe	see cheap	see she's	see cheese	see sheep
21.	tiny	toes	teen	stay	toys	tiny
22.	go	do	to	go	gold	good
23.	set	sit	sets	sat	set	sell
24.	hold	gold	help	sold	told	hold
25.	is she	is shy	is his	is her	she is	is she

Exercise 44. Intermediate

1.	bit	but	bat	bet	bit	tab
2.	lived in	live in	alive in	living in	lived in	loved in
3.	cry	dry	say	try	cry	cob
4.	fish	find	feel	wish	fish	fine
5.	heat	help	heat	hear	heard	keep
6.	train	rain	raise	tree	tray	train
7.	coat	cold	code	coat	coats	coast
8.	that fork	that fish	that dark	that fake	that fork	that fake
9.	washer	washing	rewash	washes	washed	washer
10.	slowly	slows	lowly	slowly	only	slow
11.	cats	cat	caps	cars	cats	cans
12.	an ear	an even	an oar	a tear	an ear	a fear
13.	dine on	died on	don't on	done on	dine on	dining on
14.	am	at	an	and	ant	am
15.	the pencil	the pens	the pencil	the pencils	the pen	the prince
16.	under	uncle	below	above	only	under
17.	if she'll	if shells	if she's	she should	if she'll	she shouldn't
18.	chair	share	cheese	cheap	chair	care
19.	can't	can't	cannot	can	could	couldn't
20.	I might	I light	one night	a right	I might	I sigh
21.	music	loose	mouse	music	meals	noodle
22.	sort	store	sore	tore	sort	sure
23.	we found	we find	we found	we finish	we fear	we fool
24.	with	wish	which	with	without	witch
25.	juice	young	you're	yours	juice	junior

Exercise 45. Intermediate

1.	to stop	to spot	to stop	to rot	to shoot	to opt
2.	the class	the clash	the close	the claps	the clasp	the class
3.	ash	she	fish	lash	mash	ash
4.	cheat	cheap	chip	sheet	cheat	sheep
5.	break	brake	black	break	broke	brick
6.	big branch	big block	big blast	big black	big change	big branch
7.	know	known	knew	won	none	know
8.	done	dome	done	bone	dune	don
9.	deer	peer	deep	beer	deer	deed
10.	at least	list at	lost at	at least	less at	at last
11.	two pines	two pins	two pines	two spins	two bins	two pounds
12.	sole	loss	loose	lost	sold	sole
13.	choose	choose	shoes	shows	hoes	shops
14.	lunch	hunch	lurch	lunch	punch	launch
15.	chose	chore	core	shore	shows	chose
16.	the ropes	the robes	the drops	the ropes	the trips	the pores
17.	hall	fall	tall	gall	laugh	hall
18.	seed	seed	speed	sped	deer	speak
19.	white beard	white bird	white bread	white beards	white beard	white birds
20.	chess	cheese	choose	crease	chess	cheats
21.	tail	tile	tail	tire	tide	till
22.	swamp	swing	swipe	swamp	swamps	swipes
23.	larvae	lava	larvae	early	lonely	loudly
24.	see the test	take a taste	they tossed	see the toast	see the task	see the test
25.	shape	ship	shape	chip	chop	each

Exercise 46. Intermediate

1. after	fatter	after	affect	raft	taffy
2. ever	every	never	even	ever	seven
3. wanted to	wanting to	wants to	unwanted in	wanted to	want to
4. alone	lonely	aloud	alone	one	tore
5. under	utter	udder	sudden	upper	under
6. in front	in front	in fried	afraid of	in four	friend in
7. eager	gear	grease	aged	beagle	eager
8. is iron	is wrong	is irony	is ironic	is iron	is ironed
9. over	rove	over	revert	clover	overt
10. area	ears	are	areas	early	area
11. your teeth	your tooth	your feet	your foot	your teeth	you've taken
12. east	tease	east	seat	ease	steal
13. point	points	paint	point	paints	pants
14. obey	boy	okay	elbow	yours	obey
15. was upset	was absent	was upset	is absent	is upset	is up to me
16. cork	cute	corks	core	cuter	cork
17. shape	shop	sharp	ship	sheep	shape
18. a branch	a lunch	a beach	a ranch	a branch	a brake
19. lays	plays	laws	toys	law	lays
20. they use	they sue	they sued	they used	they're usual	they use
21. age	cage	ago	gear	page	age
22. an empty one	a pretty one	an easy one	an angry one	an entire one	an empty one
23. image	image	imagine	game	images	make
24. wings	winds	swings	wing	paints	wings
25. broad	road	proud	broad	roads	brown

Exercise 47. Intermediate

1. yellow	mellow	jello	fellow	hello	yellow
2. rock in	rock in	lock in	flock in	clock in	block in
3. best	vest	best	west	chest	nest
4. this house	this mouse	these shoes	this hose	this house	these houses
5. ladder	latter	letter	ladder	better	patter
6. a van	a vent	a van	a ban	a can	a cane
7. bread	bread	read	bead	dread	hear
8. not to slide	not a lid	not to hide	not to the side	not to lie	not to slide
9. lays	lays	aisle	hay	last	lay
10. clock	clock	lock	block	luck	lack
11. gun	fun	gun	pun	run	bun
12. the hammer	the ham	the jam	the hammer	the mammal	the lame
13. shirt	shirts	skirt	skirts	shirt	hurt
14. market	marker	marked	market	marks	target
15. moon	coon	noon	soon	gnome	moon
16. a big jar	a big gun	a big car	a big jar	a big yard	a big car
17. wool	wore	week	wool	wheel	cool
18. man	name	am	men	man	ham
19. a new tie	now die	a new tie	now lie	a new pie	again lied
20. rot	shot	lot	hot	pot	rot
21. punch	punch	punches	punching	punched	pound
22. zip	zap	tax	zipper	spits	zip
23. pan	pin	pen	pan	pun	pond
24. a flag	a flag	a flake	a flat	a page	a leg
25. tree	three	tree	true	tray	trek

Exercise 48. Intermediate

1. shed	shore	herd	head	shed	shapes
2. brush	hush	rush	such	brush	push
3. the flag	the flag	the lag	the laugh	the tag	the rag
4. to carry	to marry	to carve	to care	to cure	to carry
5. paper	people	pulpit	pupil	caper	paper
6. gum	gun	game	gum	bum	rum
7. purple	pocket	pillow	puppy	purple	pulse
8. not gray	not gray	not grey	not grow	not grab	not green
9. pop	pot	pop	bob	pen	top
10. sink in	sink in	sank in	pink in	think in	sin in
11. white	wait	while	white	which	when
12. arm	share	mar	ram	arm	lamb
13. roll	roll	rolls	toll	tolls	real
14. top	toss	mop	pot	opt	top
15. to load	too loud	to beat	to look	to lend	to load
16. one	ore	gone	run	one	ton
17. red	read	red	ready	bed	lead
18. four	door	flour	four	seal	found
19. lift	lift	felt	left	lifted	lifts
20. I saw	I sat	I was	I saw	I say	I stay
21. star	stir	star	start	tar	tars
22. and sock	and seek	and socket	and rock	and sack	and sock
23. feet	feat	feed	feed	feast	feet
24. grave	great	gravy	grave	grow	ground
25. ten eggs	the egg	ten eggs	ten bags	two eggs	the end

Exercise 49. Intermediate

1. fence	fence	hence	tense	chance	fend
2. pink	think	pink	mink	thin	sink
3. on the roof	in the root	on the roof	in the food	on the road	on the route
4. rain	ram	refrain	train	rein	rain
5. eight or	ate or	free or	eggs or	eight or	fight or
6. nest	neat	rest	next	nest	best
7. your nose	your rose	your nice	your house	your noisy	your nose
8. stamps	maps	storms	stamp	stamps	strong
9. stick	stack	tick	stitch	stick	stuck
10. out of ten	ten of	often	out of tin	out of ten	of tin
11. truck	track	trick	truck	tuck	tract
12. nurse	nuns	nuisance	under	sudden	nurse
13. not a table	not a table	not a tube	not able	not a tablet	not time
14. hen	then	hen	hint	her	hell
15. nine	nice	find	nip	nine	wine
16. fail	sail	flail	jail	faint	fail
17. ball	tall	hat	bell	bald	ball
18. fan	far	fun	fan	ban	fin
19. don't split	don't spill	don't spit	don't spell	don't splash	don't split
20. frog	hog	free	frog	fragile	afraid
21. hand	hand	had	hen	band	hard
22. one dollar	one follower	one dealer	hollow	one seller	one dollar
23. hat	halt	hot	had	hat	bad
24. one dime	one dome	one dead	one dim	one dire	one dime
25. cough	caught	fought	couch	cough	coughed

Exercise 50. Intermediate

1. alpaca	alpha	pack	alpaca	clap	scalp
2. a large boa	a large boar	a large book	a large bow	a large boat	a large boa
3. camel	came	camel	clam	mace	game
4. duck	dud	cluck	puck	dunk	duck
5. an eagle	a beagle	an eager	a league	an ugly	an eagle
6. fly	flu	ply	fly	folly	lye
7. gull	lug	gull	gulp	plug	glum
8. a horse	a hearse	a shore	a rose	a horse	a hose
9. scratch	scream	catch	catches	screen	scratch
10. koala	cola	kites	coping	koala	cover
11. llama	mama	lame	llama	mall	llamas
12. to pretend	to repeat	too pretty	to believe	to protect	to pretend
13. monkey	monk	monkey	money	yellow	keys
14. they chase	they change	they cheat	they charge	they chase	they hasten
15. puppy	under	bubble	poppy	peppy	puppy
16. violin	urchin	volatile	voiced	violin	violent
17. turtle	reptile	testing	turned	turtle	dirtier
18. those eraser	those easy	those mistakes	those pencils	those early	those erasers
19. rabbit	rabid	rapid	rabbit	tribute	rancid
20. a whole	a whale	a white	a hole	a whole	a wallet
21. table	paper	butter	able	cable	table
22. someone	sometime	someday	ones	someone	sorry
23. rail	trail	sell	rain	rail	learn
24. boats	boast	vote	baste	boat	boats
25. and shoes	and chews	and shoots	and shops	and shoes	and toes

Exercise 51. Intermediate

1. all the juice	all the jokes	all the yeast	all the young	all the juicy	all the juice
2. lake	take	kale	lake	tale	like
3. they laugh	they laugh	their graph	they're ugly	they're glad	she laughs
4. meat	eat	team	meant	meat	meal
5. nasal	nasal	sane	basal	nose	lass
6. jab	jam	tab	job	bad	jab
7. karat	karat	cart	rat	rake	ark
8. to live in	to live at	to live on	to live in	to live for	to live with
9. marry	married	ram	yam	army	marry
10. near	ear	near	read	hear	eerie
11. to rob	to row	to lob	to rub	to rob	to ride
12. keep this	keep them	keep these	keep this	keep that	keep those
13. kill them	spill them	like them	kill then	like then	kill them
14. mime	mime	mine	time	mite	mined
15. one night	one might	one night	one light	one thing	one flight
16. jerk	reject	jeer	perk	jerk	yank
17. lemons	limes	leaves	melons	menus	lemons
18. love	evolve	loved	loving	love	lovely
19. mound	mount	round	nouns	moaned	mound
20. off and on	often on	on and off	offer one	off and on	off and then
21. just	jury	jest	just	juice	rust
22. lump	rump	puma	lump	lunatic	landed
23. mute	mite	mute	mutt	time	muted
24. cute	cut	cuts	cuter	cute	good
25. shave	shove	share	shape	shore	shave

Exercise 52. Intermediate

1. on the ice	on the nice	on the ace	on the rice	on the dice	on the ice
2. knock	knot	knack	knock	nick	know
3. last	list	lass	last	cast	lost
4. very low	very low	every lot	every cow	very long	every law
5. mine	mind	mane	mine	miner	name
6. mow	mop	tow	how	mow	top
7. not now	knot now	not now	not new	ton now	note now
8. ouch	ouch	couch	once	touch	our
9. pot	port	rot	pore	pot	pet
10. quite	quit	quiet	quick	quote	quite
11. huge bomb	hang by	huge book	huge box	hug the baby	huge bomb
12. tape	tube	tale	cape	tape	type
13. gym	guy	jug	join	gym	jean
14. a vest	a view	a vet	a very	a bet	a vest
15. with me	wish me	watch me	without me	with me	with my
16. I	A	Y	J	E	I
17. I yell	I fell	me yet	I get	I will	I yell
18. zoo	zoot	sue	suit	zoom	zoo
19. knew	know	known	knot	news	knew
20. net	new	nest	net	met	men
21. upon	open	up	anon	upon	once
22. mind	mine	mint	moan	many	mind
23. to quell	two quails	to quell	to swell	to quilt	a quest
24. vet	vote	jet	vet	vat	vim
25. once	pounce	one	owe	once	ounce

Exercise 53. Intermediate

1. to ask	a task	to ask	an ark	it's as	a mass
2. sole	loses	solely	lose	slow	sole
3. really quick	real quirk	really quit	real quack	really quick	really quiet
4. under	until	udder	under	undid	thunder
5. vote now	veto now	vote now	vast now	vet now	voter now
6. beak	beat	book	peak	beak	bake
7. dirt	dry	tart	dirty	dire	dirt
8. jam is	jell is	jaw is	ham is	gem is	jam is
9. grow	grew	grown	grow	throw	row
10. knead it	knew it	know it	kneads it	heard it	knead it
11. mouse	house	moose	mice	mound	mouse
12. yak	yack	yam	year	jack	yak
13. wife	whiff	wolf	wife	drift	wives
14. act	art	ace	and	tack	act
15. not allow	not at all	not let	not along	not hollow	not allow
16. doom	den	boom	door	drool	doom
17. elf	self	ear	elf	elm	tell
18. date	date	dark	dame	rate	dart
19. give them	given them	glove then	dive then	give them	gift then
20. girl	core	grit	curl	girl	grim
21. the guy	the gum	the group	the guy	the gun	the joy
22. home	hole	come	hem	hope	home
23. hear	heard	heal	shear	he	hear
24. inch	itch	ink	itchy	inches	inch
25. joy	job	join	joy	jay	boy

Exercise 54. Intermediate

1. an apple	a lapel	an apple	a label	an attack	an apron
2. beet	bean	beet	bleat	beat	tee
3. cherry	cherry	cheer	beach	hurry	yearly
4. a drink	a rink	a ring	a thing	a knot	a drink
5. egg	beg	get	edge	egg	eggs
6. some grapes	some trades	some drapes	some traps	some grapes	some grades
7. fruit	futile	fruit	fluid	fulfill	fruitful
8. ham	man	hat	jam	sham	ham
9. iced	ice	icy	ices	dice	iced
10. like jelly	like yellow	like young	like early	like jelly	like years
11. kabob	carob	bark	bob	back	kabob
12. your liver	you live	your liver	you're evil	you're vile	your river
13. meat	meat	eat	team	attempt	met
14. nuts	stun	nut	ton	nuts	not
15. orange	range	ounce	grange	orange	angle
16. peach	each	cheap	ache	patch	peach
17. plum	plummet	rummel	liver	lumber	plum
18. rum	rut	urn	rum	mum	ram
19. soup for	shop for	soup for	soap for	sound for	send for
20. tea	eat	ate	tee	tea	team
21. candy	candy	dandy	yankee	day	thank
22. many vitamins	many votes	many vases	many votes	many vitamins	many veterans
23. think	thing	sink	zinc	thin	think
24. the water	the waiter	they want	the waste	the water	they wanted
25. zucchini	chin	zealous	zippers	zucchini	spaghetti

Exercise 55. Intermediate

1. eleven	seven	eleven	even	sever	ever
2. to cry	to cry	to try	to pray	to fly	to dry
3. jump	drum	jam	jumble	bump	jump
4. comb	lamb	come	comb	numb	came
5. not a skate	not a skirt	not a shirt	not shade	not a spade	not a skate
6. store	more	core	tore	stare	store
7. fat cow	but how	and flow	for now	fat clown	fat cow
8. run	rug	run	rind	rain	rut
9. sink	think	drink	link	thing	sink
10. blue ball	very tall	in the hall	blue ball	in fall	don't call
11. sit	sit	thin	sat	set	sift
12. sleep	sweep	sleep	sheep	weep	swing
13. lip	life	lab	pill	love	lip
14. a dress	a lease	a rest	a dress	a dream	a mess
15. swim	swing	swim	limb	sweep	slim
16. your watch	your water	your watch	you walk	you wash	your wish
17. wood	good	would	flood	wood	hood
18. not blow	not glow	not slow	not blow	not low	not flow
19. sweater	swinger	linger	sweeter	sweatier	sweater
20. thumb	humble	thus	plum	thumb	lamb
21. ride	ride	wide	hide	drive	five
22. rope	cope	hop	rope	soap	grope
23. bad stain	red stone	the stair	much steam	bad stain	in Spain
24. push	plush	pushed	lush	push	flush
25. pull	pool	bull	pull	hull	push

Exercise 56. Intermediate

1. the cars	this car	three cars	ten cars	the cars	the scars
2. of	off	of	for	or	on
3. to school	to score	to schools	at school	in school	to school
4. hunt	hint	huge	hunts	hunted	hunt
5. on	on	of	for	no	by
6. off	of	for	off	top	fog
7. stop now	pots now	spot now	stop now	top now	tops now
8. carpet	paper	cars	parked	carpet	garbage
9. no beards	no birds	no beds	no bears	no beans	no beards
10. that my	had, my	this, my	hat, my	them, my	that, my
11. these	those	that	this	these	then
12. those	hoses	hostess	these	those	then
13. is	in	it	is	id	if
14. are	area	ear	real	tar	are
15. war was	wars were	war was	raw was	saw was	wasp was
16. were	where	here	when	were	work
17. be	bee	beet	am	is	be
18. am next	and next	a nest	are next	am next	ax next
19. club	clap	clubs	cub	club	calf
20. able	album	ability	camel	able	aren't
21. tennis then	tent then	sent then	ten is then	finish then	tennis then
22. down	pound	own	sound	down	downs
23. in	it	is	in	if	id
24. have seen	have knees	have seeds	have been	have said	have seen
25. your pocket	your rocker	your rocket	your socket	your pocket	your knock

■ Exercise 57. Intermediate

1. fix	fits	fit	fix	fins	fish
2. real ark	real art	real ark	real tar	really ask	really asked
3. grass	rags	grabs	rag	brass	grass
4. an eel	an ill	an owl	an early	an eel	a peel
5. hill	dill	hill	bill	pill	sill
6. barn	ran	ban	bran	barn	barns
7. foxes	knocks	boxes	facts	fox	foxes
8. with a doll	with dill	with a tool	with a deal	with a doll	with dull
9. apron	upon	pun	apron	prone	apart
10. horse	house	coarse	hoarse	worse	horse
11. and goats	and floats	and goats	and got	and gets	and most
12. insect	excite	excited	section	inspect	insect
13. my dog	my good	my dogs	my goal	my dog	my day
14. farm	farm	form	harm	forms	arm
15. the path	the paths	the pots	the past	the path	the post
16. boat	boat	boot	beet	boats	bet
17. donkey	keys	monkey	donkeys	monkeys	donkey
18. a cap	a cop	a cup	a car	a carp	a cap
19. bear	tear	veer	wear	bear	beard
20. socks	sock	sacks	rocks	stocks	socks
21. snake	rake	snake	necks	legs	hook
22. fight	light	right	bright	sight	fight
23. gloves	gloves	loves	loving	lovers	jives
24. fresh carrots	fresh carrot	five parrots	few carrots	fresh carrots	fried carrots
25. candle	handle	dances	candy	handy	candle

Exercise 58. Intermediate

1. climb	limb	climb	lamb	clam	cling
2. pie	tie	bye	vie	pie	fie
3. chick	hitch	kick	chicken	click	chick
4. your knee	your knife	you knew	your knee	your know	your key
5. pig	rig	twig	fig	pig	wig
6. pipe	pipe	ripe	pyre	wipe	like
7. kick	tick	hitch	kick	chick	click
8. a worm	a warm	an arm	a warning	adorn	a worm
9. blue	blow	blew	blue	blunt	blown
10. a bowl of	a box of	a growl from	a howl from	a bowl of	a book of
11. head	heard	head	heat	had	aid
12. brush	hush	rush	shush	bush	brush
13. to hush	to hush	to rush	too much	to push	to brush
14. broom	groom	broom	room	croon	hook
15. clown	clown	clone	lawn	round	brown
16. not a wheel	not a heel	not wheat	not peel	not when	not a wheel
17. desk	dress	desks	flask	desk	less
18. elf	shelf	elves	self	elf	help
19. a gate	a goat	a jacket	a gate	a hat	a plate
20. ink	ink	pink	think	imp	sink
21. the horn	the home	the honest	the homer	the horns	the horn
22. tail	tile	tall	tailor	tail	talent
23. jay	gay	hay	yea	jay	pay
24. jeep in	keep in	jeep in	jeeps in	keeps in	jade in
25. goose	geese	juice	oozes	goose	grease

Exercise 59. Intermediate

1. is	his	it	as	in	is
2. the laughter	the relaxing	the looking	the creature	the laughter	the laughing
3. hit	hitch	him	hilt	hit	wit
4. jewel	jewelry	jewels	jungle	jewel	juniper
5. grab	gray	grub	brag	grab	glad
6. jeans	jeer	jeans	beans	jell	joins
7. glow	grow	glob	low	blow	glow
8. in a box	in an ox	ink box	it's a box	sin in a	in a box
9. find the	the hind	the fine	fire the	find the	fund the
10. flood	flood	fled	blood	door	flowed
11. hose	house	host	used	hose	nose
12. got	get	gore	god	tug	got
13. it	it	sit	in	if	hit
14. I hold	I held	I hold	I'm bold	I had	I helped
15. front	font	flaunt	fled	front	runt
16. junk in	just in	put in	junk in	not in	judge in
17. jaw	wage	wag	jab	paw	jaw
18. from	farm	trauma	front	from	form
19. harm	harem	ram	hard	harm	harness
20. I'm ill	I'm all	I'll ask	I'm ill	I'm late	I'm past
21. grip	trip	rip	grip	pig	grope
22. jack	jock	yank	junk	joke	jack
23. this game	these gems	this gem	this game	these games	this gas
24. hail	laid	hail	hell	hall	hull
25. an iron	an early	an icon	a ruin	the irony	an iron

Exercise 60. Intermediate

1. quill	quirk	guilt	quince	quiet	quill
2. sled to	slide to	lead to	led to	sled to	said to
3. uniform	form	uniform	unicorn	unicycle	acorns
4. web	wet	ebb	rib	wed	web
5. is a parrot	is parting	is a carrot	is a parrot	is parted	is a part
6. ape	apt	cape	ate	pea	ape
7. tepee	tepid	petro	peat	tepee	tallow
8. and would	and wood	and should	and could	and would	and wound
9. quart	garter	quarter	heart	guard	quart
10. window	winded	follow	wound	window	windows
11. a train	a train	a random	a rainy	a trained	a treaty
12. pear	pears	ear	hear	pair	pear
13. violin is	violet is	varnish is	violin is	viola is	vile is
14. puppet	peeling	puppy	purest	puppet	punish
15. across	cross	crossed	acorn	across	afront
16. wood	good	hood	food	wood	wand
17. tiger	teem	team	tagged	tiger	repeat
18. the river	the arrival	the arrivals	the night	the rivers	the river
19. toys	stay	stays	guys	toys	toyed
20. umbrella	uncles	under	amber	umbrella	jumping
21. above it	under it	after it	about it	above it	below it
22. rings	string	strings	thing	sling	rings
23. any time	many times	any time	little time	no time	my time
24. part	parts	art	parted	paint	part
25. truck	drunk	frock	shuck	truck	struck

■ *Exercise 61. Intermediate*

1. jam	join	jeans	jam	ham	ram
2. leaves	leaf	leave	lives	leaves	leaven
3. key	keys	keep	quart	key	keen
4. on the map	on the mop	on the stamp	in the pen	on the map	on the maps
5. moon	noon	moon	loom	room	goon
6. knife	kneel	kind	nifty	kinds	knife
7. and milk	and cream	and water	and sugar	and meat	and milk
8. lamp	palm	lamp	light	plant	loom
9. kettle	kitchen	kites	kitten	kettle	nettle
10. the nest	the best	the vest	the nest	the mess	the feast
11. oar	our	boar	roar	oar	out
12. money	many	change	moon	meaning	money
13. several oaks	seven oaks	several oars	severe case	several oaks	seven locks
14. log	long	log	goal	loud	dog
15. king	kinds	king	queen	kind	kings
16. he owed	he wed	he owned	he bowed	he owed	he downed
17. needle	needed	nibble	needle	neared	kneaded
18. music	musical	mustard	music	must	muse
19. a lamb	a limb	a lumber	a palm	a lamb	a plan
20. oven	cover	owned	owed	oven	hover
21. a big lion	a big leaf	a big lean	a big lion	big lions	a big lazy
22. kite	kitten	kite	caught	kind	kit
23. park	perk	pink	parked	park	parks
24. paint	paint	painting	parted	parting	pain
25. two kittens	two kittens	two kitchens	two kids	two kinder	two kits

Exercise 62. Intermediate

1. renew	revolve	anew	renew	newer	raven
2. chalk	hat	hulk	chalk	change	heart
3. drown	drove	frown	brown	crown	drown
4. beat	bear	heat	deaf	beat	beaten
5. a door	a boar	a bore	a door	adorn	and four
6. our annual	our annual	our last	our new	our nail	our lane
7. to enter	to return	to exit	to turn	to enter	to center
8. dripping	tripping	dipping	tipping	dripping	gripping
9. erase it	cease it	raise it	save it	sear it	erase it
10. balcony	balloon	combine	balcony	balance	ballast
11. chew	clue	chew	few	chop	show
12. if you arrive	if arriving	if it arrives	if you arrived	if your arrival	if you arrive
13. duel	due	duke	dole	duel	duet
14. elect	erect	electric	eclectic	clench	elect
15. bribe	drive	bride	bribe	bring	brave
16. they rode	they ripen	they erode	they've ridden	the road	they rode
17. ant	ant	tan	and	gnat	neat
18. cruise	crews	druid	cleans	crumble	cruise
19. dare	dear	read	dare	raid	down
20. your pupil	your people	your puppy	your puppet	your purple	your pupil
21. danger	grange	range	ranged	danger	endanger
22. crown	drown	grown	gown	crow	crown
23. earn	penny	yearn	learned	earn	earned
24. receipt	receive	deceit	recalls	recalled	receipt
25. was bitten	was better	is bitten	was bitten	was a kitten	was bitter

Exercise 63. Intermediate

1. very brief	very bright	very light	very brown	very bad	very brief
2. slap	drape	shape	sap	lap	slap
3. put	punt	pun	put	poor	pint
4. years ago	years gone	years go	your ages	years ago	your age
5. win	wine	won	win	winter	two
6. a big bill	a big bell	a big bill	a big ball	a big bowl	a big bull
7. air	hair	air	aired	heart	stare
8. the bird	the birds	the beard	the dirt	the bird	the beards
9. front	back	fright	from	frond	front
10. ax	axe	as	so	at	ax
11. and books	and book	and books	and good	and door	and goods
12. band	bank	band	bond	bad	bend
13. block	black	bleak	blown	block	crock
14. am	an	ma	as	am	is
15. start	store	stored	started	starts	start
16. box, and	rocks, and	fox, and	ox, and	box, and	stocks, and
17. bath	baths	bathe	bath	tub	vats
18. brave	bravo	raven	breathe	breath	brave
19. all of	some of	most of	none of	all of	much of
20. boot	beet	bitten	but	foot	boot
21. a bag	a band	a wagon	a bag	a baggy	a bay
22. bell	ball	boll	bell	bill	belt
23. won	win	wound	won	went	want
24. the bone	the bun	the boat	the boom	the bone	the bond
25. bean	bear	been	beat	veal	bean

Exercise 64. Intermediate

1.	unit	until	tune	untie	unit	knit
2.	who did	how did	whom did	woo does	who does	who did
3.	where	when	why	which	where	here
4.	the zone	the nose	the zone	the zoo	the ozone	the noise
5.	void	avoid	dive	viola	invite	void
6.	what	hat	what	wheat	thaw	whet
7.	weed	need	meet	wed	wood	weed
8.	uncle	ankle	clunk	buckle	uncle	aunt
9.	not veal	not leave	not feel	not veal	not evil	not a vest
10.	which	watch	witch	chew	itch	which
11.	young	you	young	gnome	gong	going
12.	tame	team	time	tame	take	tan
13.	until she	until he	until I	until she	until we	until you
14.	youth	young	youth	thou	you	couth
15.	there are	these are	where are	those are	there are	they're
16.	scent	science	scientist	sent	scent	scare
17.	to visit	to sift	to vary	to vote	to visit	to invite
18.	oink	coin	oink	knock	con	oil
19.	undo	under	doing	undid	undo	done
20.	why you	why you	where you	if you	how you	what you
21.	hate yams	hate jams	hate games	hate yams	hate maps	hate mops
22.	ugliness	treatment	prettier	thereby	umbrella	ugliness
23.	whoever	whomever	whenever	whose	wholesome	whoever
24.	zero	cereal	hero	rose	zero	erode
25.	fuel	feel	full	fool	fuel	fail

Exercise 65. Intermediate

1. can't	can	tan	can't	won't	pants
2. tough	fought	tough	teach	tears	taint
3. ghost	ghoul	ghastly	guest	tough	ghost
4. apes	peas	saps	ape	tapes	apes
5. the fifth	the five	the fire	the fifty	the fifth	the fifteen
6. only	only	alone	once	won	ugly
7. a cramp	a ramp	cramps	ramps	crams	a cramp
8. ponder	pond	wonder	ponder	pounce	pounder
9. sick	stick	sick	six	sex	kick
10. tax that	taxi that	relax that	tea that	act that	tax that
11. cage	cage	cages	age	cave	huge
12. file	fill	filler	files	find	file
13. erase	sear	eraser	erased	erase	erases
14. this sauce	this sauce	this slice	this sound	this sausage	these sauces
15. cap, and	cape, and	caps, and	cap, and	cop, and	cup, and
16. bind	blind	bend	pint	bond	bind
17. carve	carved	carve	carves	care	cared
18. it dials	it dies	it dials	it leads	it aids	it laid
19. face	farce	fake	café	face	force
20. page	pages	pays	aged	page	paid
21. dish	dish	dishes	wish	wishes	fish
22. one style	some tiles	some styles	one style	one stale	one stellar
23. way	ways	weigh	may	way	hay
24. to pinch	to pitch	to perch	to pinch	to inch	to pin
25. pays	spay	bays	days	pays	paid

Exercise 66. Intermediate

1. only	lonely	pony	once	only	ugly
2. four pages	for paper	four papers	four pages	page four	for ages
3. wave	vein	have	make	wave	waves
4. type	tap	tip	type	pie	types
5. raise	rose	roses	rays	raise	answer
6. a quiz	a quiz	a queen	a quick	a quit	a quiet
7. number	numb	bird	member	numbers	number
8. allow	lower	lowly	allow	allot	apron
9. good deed	good deeds	good deals	good deal	good deed	good day
10. correct	called	couple	correct	recount	counter
11. you look	you cook	you book	you hook	you took	you look
12. write	write	right	rights	writes	rides
13. pencil	pens	spend	expand	pencil	pounce
14. table	bleed	able	table	ability	stable
15. have one	have on	have one	have gone	have no	have any
16. circle	girls	square	circus	circles	circle
17. those birds	that bird	those herds	those sheep	those birds	the beards
18. nice	rice	mice	ice	nice	niece
19. to play	to pray	to play	to stay	to gray	to plow
20. read	ear	heard	read	reads	reading
21. tank	tank	thank	tanks	thanks	bank
22. deposit	posed	depot	deposit	propose	decide
23. to answer	to swerve	to swear	to empty	to answer	to question
24. color	red	brown	collar	colors	color
25. last	lasts	blast	mast	masts	last

Exercise 67. Intermediate

1. tank	thank	tanks	thanks	tank	tick
2. dry	day	dry	dirt	dirty	try
3. I went	I want	I won't	I went	I wonder	I wish
4. home	home	hate	hold	hole	hand
5. wife	wife	wives	life	give	tile
6. she's	shell	she'd	he's	she's	he'd
7. a lady	a tidy	a lady	a late	a shady	a load
8. hold	hill	held	told	fold	hold
9. back	buck	beg	tack	pack	back
10. how	who	hold	wow	how	hue
11. sandy, but	son, but	sunny, but	sandy, but	sinful, but	salty, but
12. sauce	sour	sauce	salt	sense	sauces
13. know if	knot if	knew if	knob if	know if	knee if
14. with	what	wit	with	we'll	wet
15. she can	he can	she can't	he can't	we can	she can
16. does	dust	does	do	don't	doer
17. not take	not tick	not taken	not take	not tape	not tack
18. saw	was	saw	sow	sat	sap
19. of you	if you	in you	at you	of you	or you
20. tie	ten	tan	tin	tip	tie
21. all of	call off	all of	old or	fall off	tall or
22. sir	sin	sir	sit	sip	sire
23. over	after	able	over	once	only
24. yes	you	young	jet	yes	get
25. niece	nest	nice	needs	nicer	niece

Exercise 68. Intermediate

1. oral	loan	oral	only	oval	opal
2. jinx	mink	jinx	link	jail	joust
3. rind	rent	lend	grind	drink	rind
4. too far	two for	too fat	two fur	too far	two fares
5. easy	yeast	east	easy	yes	year
6. bacon	coins	baked	backed	baron	bacon
7. the duke	the ducks	the duel	the duck	the dukes	the duke
8. he fried	he tried	he fired	he fried	his friend	his frown
9. mops	snob	most	mobs	noses	mops
10. that check	that clerk	your cheek	that chick	that shack	that check
11. film	fail	film	milk	fill	final
12. praise	praise	prawns	please	raised	prince
13. seize	says	sizes	seize	easy	easier
14. ant	tan	gnat	ant	and	hand
15. the grain	them again	the green	then grind	then groan	the grain
16. yells	yell	wells	yield	yells	yelps
17. crew	wreck	creep	crew	crest	crawl
18. to drain	to train	to drown	to dream	to drain	to date
19. earth	early	spear	earth	sphere	hearth
20. a quiz	a whiz	a quiz	a dizzy	a breeze	a queen
21. bless	least	less	bless	blessed	best
22. arrow	arrow	arrows	arm	arms	rows
23. sad time	sad day	sad days	sad times	sad time	sad teams
24. hole	holy	whole	hobby	body	hole
25. bead	bead	able	tide	beat	abet

Exercise 69. Intermediate

1. leaf	leave	feel	tail	feet	leaf
2. clean air	clear air	cloud and	clean air	close and	clean are
3. hot	hot	hat	hit	hut	hop
4. windy	winds	wind	wound	windy	watery
5. the soil	they said	the soil	the seal	the soul	they sulk
6. cloud	clear	claim	cloud	clads	gloat
7. blue	bulge	bulk	blew	blue	blow
8. and cleans	and claims	and clean	and crews	and cleans	and claim
9. fresh	frail	fresh	French	frogs	frugal
10. pretty	petty	potted	peeled	pegged	pretty
11. fast	fast	fuss	ghost	fade	joust
12. beach	birch	beech	beach	bench	peach
13. not sand	not sound	not send	not sent	not sand	not sane
14. cot if	cut if	cat if	cute if	cot if	cod if
15. water	waist	waste	water	wetter	wished
16. eats	eats	eat	tea	teas	ate
17. two dogs	two days	the dogs	two dips	the days	two dogs
18. wave	wove	wave	weave	waves	weaves
19. ocean	motion	ocean	notion	icing	occult
20. fun	fan	fin	tan	fun	tuna
21. a noise	a nasty	a nearby	a nurse	a noise	a moist
22. splash	spleen	trash	splash	spits	lashes
23. radio	raided	radio	raider	rodeo	ruder
24. to chair	to share	to choose	to cheat	to shape	to chair
25. fish	fashion	fresh	fish	lash	touch

Exercise 70. Intermediate

1. tank	dink	tung	tank	thank	thin
2. auto	oats	autos	auto	oat	toast
3. belt	bell	felt	belt	melt	pelt
4. to cost	to most	to scold	to cost	to coat	to toast
5. need it	near it	meet it	veto it	lead it	need it
6. of all	at all	on all	up all	in all	of all
7. just	just	gust	jest	must	gist
8. might	night	might	right	sight	tight
9. cuts	cute	cut	guts	cuts	gut
10. furry	funny	furry	money	hurry	bunny
11. what	wheat	whiz	when	wharf	what
12. I would	I should	I could	I would	I will	I won't
13. felt	felt	feel	belt	bend	fend
14. vein	veto	vein	vane	vine	voice
15. your town	your turn	your loan	your town	your team	your tour
16. led	lid	lad	load	led	lead
17. is alive	is aloof	was alive	is alien	was aloof	is alive
18. either	also	neither	ether	either	too
19. allow	lowly	alter	allow	aloof	afloat
20. higher	high	higher	highest	hugest	height
21. had eaten	had eaten	has eaten	have eaten	was eaten	are eaten
22. sour	sod	said	sued	sad	sour
23. sad	sod	said	sued	sad	sadder
24. shine	shone	chime	shine	shame	chore
25. good union	good onion	good uncle	good unit	good unions	good union

Exercise 71. Advanced (Academic Word List)

1. approximated	accommodation	acknowledged	administration	approximated	automatically
2. consistent	challenge	concurrent	confirmed	constraint	consistent
3. financial	financial	flexibility	formula	founded	functional
4. legal	labor	license	layer	legal	lecture
5. sector	section	sector	select	similar	solely
6. assessment	anticipated	appreciation	amendment	assessment	assistance
7. commission	components	commenced	commission	commitment	constitution
8. percent	percent	parallel	passive	primary	priority
9. policy	policy	passive	posed	primary	pursue
10. evidence	enhance	equation	evidence	excluded	exposure
11. error	ethic	exceed	erode	error	equip
12. alternative	assessment	amendment	analogous	ambiguous	alternative
13. implies	ignored	implies	implicit	indicate	induced
14. code	cycle	credit	code	create	confirm
15. theory	target	theory	thesis	topics	trendy
16. authority	arbitrary	assembly	assigned	available	authority
17. contact	convert	convince	converse	contact	contrast
18. source	solely	sought	source	sphere	status
19. security	security	specific	stability	statistics	survive
20. focus	focus	format	founded	function	funds
21. income	implicit	income	indicate	induced	integral
22. credit	create	chart	cited	civil	credit
23. required	retained	required	revealed	rejected	removed
24. entities	estates	exports	extracts	ensures	entities
25. expert	ethical	exhibit	expert	export	extract

12

■ Exercise 72. Advanced (Academic Word List)

1. factors	federal	formula	functions	factors	features
2. strategies	statistics	simulation	strategies	summary	structures
3. criteria	couple	crucial	criteria	culture	clarity
4. environment	enforcement	exploitation	established	environment	encountered
5. items	bias	jobs	levy	links	items
6. transfer	technical	temporary	thereby	transfer	transport
7. research	reaction	research	resident	retained	revenue
8. consequences	compensation	comprehensive	consequences	constitutional	contemporary
9. participation	participation	phenomenon	practitioners	presumption	professional
10. facilitate	facilitate	features	financial	formula	function
11. integration	inhibition	innovation	inspection	integration	interaction
12. sought	section	sphere	survive	sought	source
13. features	factors	features	federal	founded	functions
14. select	section	sector	similar	solely	select
15. available	arbitrary	assembly	assigned	authority	available
16. role	deny	role	bias	code	data
17. enhanced	elements	economic	enhanced	empirical	enormous
18. significant	significant	somewhat	sequences	similarities	statistics
19. contrast	complex	coincide	collapse	constant	contrast
20. positive	positive	potential	primary	priority	process
21. apparent	accurate	adjacent	appendix	assigned	apparent
22. lecture	journal	liberal	lecture	license	federal
23. estimate	equation	estimate	evidence	exposure	external
24. site	seek	site	bias	deny	task
25. range	range	radical	refine	rigid	route

18

Exercise 73. Advanced (Academic Word List)

1. appropriate	adjustment	ambiguous	anticipated	appropriate	assessment
2. legislation	interaction	legislation	intervention	investment	justification
3. categories	categories	challenge	coherence	colleagues	comments
4. established	enforcement	exploitation	established	environment	encountered
5. consumer	chemical	comprise	computer	corporate	consumer
6. administration	approximated	accommodation	acknowledged	administration	automatically
7. method	medical	medium	method	military	network
8. compensation	compensation	concentration	consequences	constitutional	contemporary
9. interpretation	infrastructure	interpretation	investigation	integration	interaction
10. comments	categories	chemicals	colleagues	community	comments
11. professional	perspective	practitioners	preliminary	presumption	professional
12. legal	labor	license	legal	layer	lecture
13. civil	cease	chart	cited	civil	couple
14. similar	status	similar	survive	sustain	symbol
15. approach	advocate	allocate	approach	appendix	arbitrary
16. indicate	indicate	inherent	instance	institute	integrity
17. occur	offset	option	output	access	occur
18. focus	bias	fees	files	funds	focus
19. response	relevant	required	research	response	retained
20. status	sphere	status	seeks	source	sphere
21. specific	security	stability	specific	statistics	survive
22. strategies	statistics	strategies	simulation	summary	structures
23. economic	economic	eliminate	enhanced	evolution	financial
24. distribution	distribution	demonstrate	dimensions	diminished	discretion
25. function	formats	formula	founded	function	finalizes

2 /

Exercise 74. Advanced (Academic Word List)

1. procedure	procedure	preceding	predicted	prospect	protocol
2. data	code	deny	draft	bias	data
3. legal	labor	license	layer	legal	lecture
4. physical	parallel	potential	physical	prospect	protocol
5. formula	financial	flexibility	formula	founded	functional
6. partnership	parameters	partnership	perspective	philosophy	preliminary
7. concept	complex	collapse	constant	concept	contact
8. period	parallel	passive	primary	pursue	period
9. income	implicit	income	indicate	induced	integral
10. transfer	technical	temporary	thereby	transfer	transport
11. challenge	categories	channels	challenge	chemical	coincide
12. deduction	deduction	definition	deviation	discretion	distinction
13. revealed	relevant	required	revealed	revenue	reverse
14. process	process	passive	positive	primary	purchase
15. fees	bias	files	focus	funds	fees
16. previous	potential	promote	previous	prospect	protocol
17. final	factor	final	finite	focus	funds
18. survey	status	survive	sustain	survey	symbol
19. option	offset	output	access	occur	option
20. decline	debate	decline	despite	display	domain
21. principle	principle	paragraph	perceived	persistent	predicted
22. derived	derived	detected	devoted	denoted	debated
23. benefit	behalf	benefit	debate	denote	detect
24. series	section	sector	select	series	solely
25. attitudes	analysis	accurate	arbitrary	attached	attitudes

14

Exercise 75. Advanced (Academic Word List)

1. method	medical	medium	method	military	network
2. export	ethical	exhibit	expert	export	extract
3. constitutional	consequences	considerable	constitutional	construction	consultation
4. parameters	parameters	perspective	philosophy	preliminary	professional
5. acquisition	acquisition	adaptation	aggregate	allocation	alternative
6. components	computers	consequences	constitutional	components	construction
7. financial	financial	flexibility	formula	founded	functional
8. create	civil	credit	create	chart	cited
9. community	concentration	community	considerable	constitutional	construction
10. resources	resolution	resources	responses	restraints	revolution
11. assessment	appropriate	assessment	assistance	assurance	anticipated
12. mechanism	maximum	minimized	monitoring	mechanism	motivation
13. conduct	complex	coincide	conduct	constant	comprise
14. derived	derived	detected	devoted	denoted	debated
15. normal	mutual	neutral	notion	normal	nuclear
16. individual	innovation	investment	identified	illustrated	individual
17. restricted	reinforced	resolution	restricted	registered	revealed
18. required	retained	revealed	rejected	removed	required
19. variables	variables	widespread	violation	virtually	voluntary
20. aware	access	adults	affect	author	aware
21. achieve	abstract	achieve	aspects	attained	accurate
22. consistent	construction	consequences	considerable	constitutional	consistent
23. domestic	document	domestic	dominant	dramatic	dynamic
24. credit	create	chart	cited	civil	credit
25. assume	accurate	achieve	aspects	assume	assure

Exercise 76. Advanced (Academic Word List)

1. legislation	interaction	intervention	investment	justification	legislation
2. area	access	adult	aid	alter	area
3. journal	granted	parallel	potential	project	journal
4. policy	passive	posed	primary	pursue	policy
5. research	reaction	research	resident	retained	revenue
6. authority	arbitrary	assembly	assigned	authority	available
7. role	deny	bias	code	role	data
8. distinction	depression	discretion	distinction	distortion	document
9. definition	definition	deduction	distortion	distinction	document
10. sought	source	section	sphere	sought	survive
11. conclusion	concentrate	conclusion	considerate	constitution	construction
12. estimate	equation	evidence	exposure	estimate	external
13. image	image	impact	injury	insert	issues
14. consent	concept	conflict	consent	contact	context
15. assistance	appropriate	assessment	assistance	assurance	anticipated
16. passive	period	parallel	primary	pursue	passive
17. method	medical	medium	method	military	network
18. design	debate	denote	design	device	display
19. commission	commission	conclusion	considerate	constitution	construction
20. context	contact	context	concept	conduct	conflict
21. internal	inferred	internal	invoked	involved	isolated
22. select	section	sector	similar	select	solely
23. identified	identified	illustrated	investment	innovation	integration
24. occupational	occupational	encountered	enforcement	environment	exploitation
25. evaluation	economic	evaluation	expansion	equipment	equivalent

23

Exercise 77. Advanced (Academic Word List)

1. regulations	reinforced	regulations	resources	restraints	revolution
2. definition	definition	deduction	distortion	distinction	document
3. perceived	perceived	predicted	promoted	published	purchased
4. section	solely	similar	sector	section	select
5. environment	enforcement	exploitation	established	environment	encountered
6. interaction	integration	innovation	inspection	integration	interaction
7. traditional	techniques	traditional	transition	transport	temporary
8. purchase	process	passive	purchase	positive	primary
9. participation	participation	phenomenon	practitioners	presumption	professional
10. legal	labor	license	layer	legal	lecture
11. range	radical	range	refine	rigid	route
12. validity	vehicle	validity	version	visible	volume
13. cited	cease	chart	cited	civil	clause
14. relevant	retained	revealed	relevant	removed	required
15. response	relevant	required	research	response	retained
16. categories	categories	challenge	coherence	colleagues	comments
17. positive	positive	potential	primary	priority	process
18. construction	concentration	conclusion	considerate	constitution	construction
19. dominant	document	domestic	dominant	dramatic	dynamic
20. external	equation	estimate	evidence	exposure	external
21. approach	advocate	allocation	appendix	approach	arbitrary
22. theory	target	trendy	thesis	topics	theory
23. cultural	complex	contract	contrary	contrast	cultural
24. major	mature	major	media	norms	notion
25. resident	reaction	research	resident	retained	revenue

Exercise 78. Advanced (Academic Word List)

1. formula	financial	formula	flexibility	founded	functional
2. structure	structure	summary	stability	statistics	strategy
3. available	arbitrary	assembly	assigned	authority	available
4. established	enforcement	established	exploitation	environment	encountered
5. percent	passive	primary	priority	percent	parallel
6. elements	elements	enhanced	economic	empirical	enormous
7. implications	immigration	implications	intelligence	intervention	innovation
8. method	medical	medium	method	military	network
9. administration	accommodation	acknowledged	administration	approximated	automatically
10. overall	obvious	ongoing	output	overall	overlap
11. concept	complex	collapse	constant	concept	contact
12. attributed	adequate	aggregate	allocation	analogous	attributed
13. considerable	concentration	considerate	considerable	constitution	construction
14. issue	image	impact	injury	insert	issue
15. site	seek	site	bias	deny	task
16. imposed	imposed	induced	inferred	invoked	involved
17. injury	image	impact	income	initial	injury
18. transfer	transfer	technical	temporary	thereby	transport
19. text	tapes	task	team	text	trace
20. emphasis	eliminate	emerged	emphasis	empirical	enormous
21. contract	context	concept	contrast	contract	contact
22. occur	offset	option	output	access	occur
23. complex	complex	coincide	collapse	constant	comprise
24. create	civil	credit	create	chart	cited
25. labor	hence	labor	tense	trace	legal

Exercise 79. Advanced (Academic Word List)

1. approach	advocate	allocation	appendix	approach	arbitrary
2. evidence	enhance	equation	evidence	excluded	exposure
3. affect	access	adults	affect	author	aware
4. computer	complex	computer	collapse	constant	comprise
5. corporate	corporate	chemical	comprise	computer	consumer
6. context	contact	context	concept	conduct	conflict
7. factors	federal	formula	functions	factors	features
8. commission	components	commenced	commission	commitment	constitution
9. proportion	portion	preceding	procedure	published	proportion
10. statistics	significant	somewhat	sequences	similarities	statistics
11. similar	status	similar	survive	sustain	symbol
12. despite	debate	decline	despite	display	domain
13. maintenance	manipulation	monitoring	nevertheless	maintenance	nonetheless
14. modified	modified	marginal	mediation	monitored	motivation
15. exposure	equation	evolution	expansion	exposure	evidence
16. significant	significant	somewhat	sequences	similarities	statistics
17. focus	fees	funds	focus	format	founded
18. specific	security	specific	stability	statistics	survive
19. achieve	abstract	achieve	aspects	attained	accurate
20. exceed	enable	energy	erosion	exceed	exhibit
21. restricted	restricted	reinforced	resolution	registered	revealed
22. construction	concentration	conclusion	considerate	constitution	construction
23. cycle	cycle	credit	code	create	confirm
24. benefit	behalf	denote	detect	debate	benefit
25. primary	passive	period	parallel	pursue	primary

Exercise 80. Advanced (Academic Word List)

1. period	passive	period	parallel	primary	pursue
2. assistance	appropriate	assessment	assurance	anticipated	assistance
3. procedure	procedure	preceding	predicted	prospect	protocol
4. convention	convention	conclusion	considerate	constitution	construction
5. implementation	infrastructure	interpretation	investigation	implementation	interaction
6. distribution	demonstrate	dimensions	diminished	discretion	distribution
7. economic	economic	eliminate	enhanced	evolution	financial
8. interpretation	infrastructure	interpretation	investigation	integration	interaction
9. policy	posed	primary	pursue	policy	passive
10. authority	arbitrary	assembly	assigned	authority	available
11. indicate	indicate	inherent	instance	institute	integrity
12. range	radical	range	refine	rigid	route
13. hypothesis	guidelines	hypothesis	legislation	generation	illustrated
14. version	validity	vehicle	version	visible	volume
15. source	solely	sought	source	sphere	status
16. investment	identified	illustrated	investment	innovation	integration
17. sought	sought	source	section	sphere	survive
18. legal	labor	license	layer	legal	lecture
19. select	section	sector	select	similar	solely
20. equation	evolution	expansion	exposure	equation	evidence
21. previous	potential	previous	promote	prospect	protocol
22. survey	status	survive	sustain	symbol	survey
23. design	debate	denote	design	device	display
24. domain	debate	decline	despite	display	domain
25. reaction	research	resident	retained	revenue	reaction

Exercise 81. Advanced (Academic Word List)

1. principle	principle	paragraph	perceived	persistent	predicted
2. process	process	passive	positive	primary	purchase
3. data	deny	draft	bias	code	data
4. enforcement	exploitation	established	enforcement	environment	encountered
5. traditional	techniques	traditional	transition	transport	temporary
6. approach	advocate	allocation	appendix	approach	arbitrary
7. acquisition	acquisition	adaptation	aggregate	allocation	alternative
8. features	actors	features	federal	founded	functions
9. contribution	conclusion	consultation	contribution	constitution	construction
10. prime	panel	phase	policy	posed	prime
11. individual	innovation	investment	individual	identified	illustrated
12. conclusion	concentrate	conclusion	considerate	constitution	construction
13. emerged	eliminate	emerged	emphasis	empirical	enormous
14. required	retained	revealed	rejected	removed	required
15. pursue	period	portion	precise	pursue	project
16. institute	indicate	inherent	instance	institute	integrity
17. injury	image	impact	income	initial	injury
18. rejected	retained	revealed	rejected	removed	required
19. retained	revealed	retained	rejected	removed	required
20. ensure	estate	export	extract	ensure	entity
21. regulations	regulations	reinforced	resources	restraints	revolution
22. credit	create	chart	cited	civil	credit
23. relevant	retained	revealed	relevant	removed	required
24. benefit	behalf	denote	detect	benefit	debate
25. incentive	incentive	incidence	inevitably	inhibition	interaction

Exercise 82. Advanced (Academic Word List)

1. constitutional	consequences	constitutional	considerable	construction	consultation
2. philosophy	parameters	perspective	philosophy	preliminary	professional
3. stress	sought	sphere	status	styles	stress
4. debate	debate	denote	design	despite	display
5. involved	inferred	internal	invoked	involved	isolated
6. factors	federal	formula	functions	factors	features
7. predicted	procedure	preceding	predicted	prospect	protocol
8. security	security	specific	stability	statistics	survive
9. available	arbitrary	assembly	assigned	authority	available
10. rational	random	rational	reaction	rejected	relaxed
11. transfer	technical	temporary	thereby	transfer	transport
12. function	formats	formula	founded	function	finalizes
13. reaction	research	resident	retained	revenue	reaction
14. participation	participation	phenomenon	practitioners	presumption	professional
15. resources	resolution	resources	responses	restraints	revolution
16. design	debate	denote	design	device	display
17. primary	passive	period	parallel	primary	pursue
18. distinction	depression	distinction	discretion	distortion	document
19. excluded	enhance	excluded	equation	evidence	exposure
20. injury	image	impact	income	initial	injury
21. target	target	theory	thesis	topics	trendy
22. create	civil	credit	create	chart	cited
23. capable	chapter	chemical	clarity	clauses	capable
24. definition	definition	deduction	distortion	distinction	document
25. initial	impact	income	initial	injury	image

Exercise 83. Advanced (Academic Word List)

1. equation	evolution	expansion	exposure	equation	evidence
2. assume	accurate	achieve	aspects	assume	assure
3. consequences	compensation	comprehensive	consequences	constitutional	contemporary
4. procedure	procedure	preceding	predicted	prospect	protocol
5. consistent	challenge	concurrent	confirmed	consistent	constraint
6. framework	fluctuations	forthcoming	framework	fundamental	furthermore
7. analysis	accurate	analysis	arbitrary	attached	attitudes
8. sector	section	sector	select	similar	solely
9. items	levy	links	items	bias	jobs
10. computer	complex	computer	collapse	constant	comprise
11. final	factor	finite	focus	funds	final
12. section	sector	select	similar	solely	section
13. context	contact	context	concept	conduct	conflict
14. positive	positive	potential	primary	priority	process
15. significant	significant	somewhat	sequences	similarities	statistics
16. issue	image	impact	injury	insert	issue
17. function	formats	formula	founded	function	finalizes
18. conduct	complex	coincide	conduct	constant	comprise
19. variables	variables	widespread	violation	virtually	voluntary
20. identified	identified	illustrated	investment	innovation	integration
21. construction	concentration	conclusion	considerate	constitution	construction
22. outcomes	objective	obtained	ongoing	outcomes	overseas
23. estimate	equation	estimate	evidence	exposure	external
24. granted	journal	parallel	granted	potential	project
25. role	deny	bias	code	data	role

Exercise 84. Advanced (Academic Word List)

1. role	deny	role	bias	code	data
2. response	relevant	required	research	response	retained
3. income	implicit	income	indicate	induced	integral
4. theory	target	theory	thesis	topics	trendy
5. select	section	sector	select	series	solely
6. categories	categories	challenge	coherence	colleagues	comments
7. corresponding	concentrating	differentiating	contemporary	corresponding	discriminating
8. policy	posed	primary	pursue	policy	passive
9. involved	inferred	internal	invoked	isolated	involved
10. assessment	anticipated	appreciation	amendment	assessment	assistance
11. accurate	achieve	aspects	assume	assure	accurate
12. link	text	link	role	deny	bias
13. assistance	appropriate	assessment	assistance	assurance	anticipated
14. conference	conference	coherence	concurrent	conformity	convention
15. enforcement	enforcement	exploitation	established	environment	encountered
16. concept	complex	collapse	constant	contact	concept
17. structure	scheme	section	similar	specific	structure
18. complex	collapse	constant	comprise	coincide	complex
19. instructions	implications	instructions	intelligence	intervention	investigation
20. relevant	retained	revealed	relevant	removed	required
21. financial	financial	flexibility	formula	founded	functional
22. chapter	chapter	chemical	clarity	clauses	capable
23. normal	mutual	neutral	normal	notion	nuclear
24. factors	federal	formula	functions	features	factors
25. source	solely	sought	source	sphere	status

Exercise 85. Advanced (Academic Word List)

1. prior	panel	phase	posed	prime	prior
2. formula	financial	flexibility	formula	founded	functional
3. marginal	modified	marginal	mediation	modified	monitored
4. authority	arbitrary	assembly	assigned	authority	available
5. survey	status	survive	sustain	symbol	survey
6. environment	enforcement	exploitation	established	environment	encountered
7. region	reveal	section	region	release	retain
8. legislation	interaction	legislation	intervention	investment	justification
9. community	commodity	conference	conferencing	community	controversy
10. similar	similar	status	survive	sustain	symbol
11. investment	interaction	legislation	intervention	investment	justification
12. percent	parallel	passive	primary	priority	percent
13. restricted	reinforced	resolution	restricted	registered	revealed
14. process	process	passive	positive	primary	purchase
15. conclusion	concentrate	conclusion	considerate	constitution	construction
16. ethnic	entities	ethical	ethnic	exhibit	explicit
17. economic	economic	eliminate	enhanced	evolution	financial
18. hence	hence	tense	thesis	trace	trend
19. equivalent	economic	equipment	equivalent	evaluation	expansion
20. contract	context	concept	contrast	contact	contract
21. potential	positive	potential	primary	priority	process
22. features	factors	features	federal	founded	functions
23. major	major	mature	media	norms	notion
24. evaluation	economic	equipment	evaluation	expansion	equivalent
25. reliance	rejected	relaxed	relevant	reliance	required

Exercise 86. Advanced (Academic Word List)

1. network	medical	medium	method	military	network
2. justification	justification	interaction	legislation	intervention	investment
3. amendment	assessment	alternative	ambiguous	amendment	analogous
4. psychology	philosophy	partnership	perspective	philosophy	psychology
5. labor	hence	tense	labor	trace	trend
6. affect	access	adults	affect	author	aware
7. distribution	distribution	demonstrate	dimensions	diminished	discretion
8. area	access	adult	aid	alter	area
9. index	image	index	injury	insert	issues
10. elements	elements	enhanced	economic	empirical	enormous
11. underlying	ultimately	underlying	undertaken	widespread	variables
12. allocation	acquisition	adaptation	aggregate	allocation	alternative
13. consistent	challenge	concurrent	confirmed	consistent	constraint
14. significant	significant	somewhat	sequences	similarities	statistics
15. coordination	consultation	contribution	coordination	controversy	cooperative
16. period	parallel	passive	primary	pursue	period
17. obvious	ongoing	obvious	output	overall	overlap
18. academic	adequate	academic	analogous	arbitrary	assistance
19. shift	shift	site	sought	sphere	stress
20. definition	distinction	document	definition	deduction	distortion
21. appropriate	adjustment	ambiguous	anticipated	appropriate	assessment
22. resources	resolution	resources	responses	restraints	revolution
23. funds	factor	final	finite	focus	funds
24. transfer	technical	temporary	thereby	transfer	transport
25. distortion	definition	deduction	distortion	distinction	document

Exercise 87. Advanced (Academic Word List)

1. range	radical	range	refine	rigid	route
2. data	deny	draft	bias	code	data
3. project	pursue	granted	period	parallel	project
4. survey	status	survey	survive	sustain	symbol
5. procedure	procedure	preceding	predicted	prospect	protocol
6. sex	job	odd	sex	sum	via
7. sector	section	sector	select	similar	solely
8. undertaken	ultimately	underlying	undertaken	widespread	variables
9. analysis	accurate	analysis	arbitrary	attached	attitudes
10. constant	complex	coincide	collapse	constant	comprise
11. strategies	simulation	summary	structures	statistics	strategies
12. principle	persistent	predicted	principle	paragraph	perceived
13. categories	categories	challenge	coherence	colleagues	comments
14. goals	focus	goals	grade	funds	hence
15. research	reaction	resident	retained	revenue	research
16. institute	indicate	inherent	instance	institute	integrity
17. ignored	ignored	implicit	implies	indicate	induced
18. positive	positive	potential	primary	priority	process
19. complex	coincide	collapse	constant	comprise	complex
20. obtained	objective	ongoing	obtained	outcomes	overseas
21. security	security	specific	stability	statistics	survive
22. involved	inferred	internal	invoked	involved	isolated
23. relevant	retained	revealed	relevant	removed	required
24. contract	context	concept	contrast	contract	contact
25. techniques	traditional	transition	transport	techniques	temporary

Exercise 88. Advanced (Academic Word List)

1. interpretation	infrastructure	interpretation	investigation	integration	interaction
2. assume	accurate	achieve	aspects	assume	assure
3. maintenance	manipulation	monitoring	nevertheless	maintenance	nonetheless
4. evidence	evidence	enhance	equation	excluded	exposure
5. conduct	complex	coincide	conduct	constant	comprise
6. administration	accommodation	acknowledged	administration	approximated	automatically
7. items	bias	jobs	levy	links	items
8. commission	components	commenced	commission	commitment	constitution
9. site	seek	site	bias	deny	task
10. occur	offset	option	output	access	occur
11. document	dominant	discretion	distinction	distortion	document
12. cultural	complex	contract	contrary	contrast	cultural
13. chapter	chapter	chemical	clarity	clauses	capable
14. variables	variables	widespread	violation	virtually	voluntary
15. sum	job	odd	sex	sum	via
16. parallel	journal	granted	journal	parallel	project
17. specific	security	statistics	survive	specific	stability
18. journal	granted	journal	parallel	potential	project
19. previous	potential	previous	promote	prospect	protocol
20. aspects	abstract	access	adults	assume	aspects
21. indicate	indicate	inherent	instance	institute	integrity
22. economic	economic	eliminate	enhanced	evolution	financial
23. structure	simulation	summary	structure	statistics	strategy
24. context	contact	context	concept	conduct	conflict
25. output	offset	option	output	access	occur

Exercise 89. Advanced (Academic Word List)

1. legislation	interaction	legislation	intervention	investment	justification
2. instance	indicate	inherent	instance	institute	integrity
3. identified	identified	illustrated	investment	innovation	integration
4. acquisition	acquisition	adaptation	aggregate	allocation	alternative
5. approach	advocate	allocation	appendix	approach	arbitrary
6. enforcement	exploitation	enforcement	established	environment	encountered
7. concentration	conclusion	considerate	constitution	construction	concentration
8. consumer	chemical	comprise	computer	corporate	consumer
9. expansion	expansion	economic	equipment	equivalent	evaluation
10. evidence	enhance	equation	evidence	excluded	exposure
11. negative	marginal	negative	nuclear	military	minimal
12. task	tapes	task	team	text	trace
13. abstract	abstract	achieve	adjacent	arbitrary	attitudes
14. summary	security	strategy	specify	summary	stability
15. assistance	appropriate	assessment	assistance	assurance	anticipated
16. region	release	retain	reveal	region	section
17. individual	innovation	investment	identified	illustrated	individual
18. layer	label	labor	layer	legal	logic
19. furthermore	fluctuations	forthcoming	framework	fundamental	furthermore
20. sequence	significant	somewhat	sequence	specific	statistics
21. gender	gender	global	grade	granted	journal
22. affect	access	adults	author	affect	aware
23. credit	create	chart	cited	civil	credit
24. regime	refine	regime	region	restore	reverse
25. major	norms	notion	mature	major	media

Exercise 90. Advanced (Academic Word List)

1. export	ethical	exhibit	expert	export	extract
2. evaluation	economic	equipment	equivalent	evaluation	expansion
3. income	implicit	income	indicate	induced	integral
4. consequences	compensation	comprehensive	consequences	constitutional	contemporary
5. assessment	assessment	alternative	ambiguous	amendment	analogous
6. reaction	research	resident	reaction	retained	revenue
7. theory	target	thesis	topics	trendy	theory
8. text	tapes	task	team	text	trace
9. research	reaction	research	resident	retained	revenue
10. site	seek	site	bias	deny	task
11. achieve	accurate	aspects	assume	assure	achieve
12. significant	significant	somewhat	sequences	similarities	statistics
13. impact	impact	income	initial	injury	image
14. rational	random	rational	reaction	rejected	relaxed
15. registered	reinforced	resolution	restricted	registered	revealed
16. trace	tapes	task	team	text	trace
17. computer	complex	collapse	constant	comprise	computer
18. tapes	tapes	task	team	text	trace
19. specified	sequence	somewhat	specific	specified	symbolic
20. normal	mutual	neutral	normal	notion	nuclear
21. job	job	odd	sex	sum	via
22. required	retained	revealed	required	rejected	removed
23. enhanced	elements	economic	empirical	enormous	enhanced
24. obtained	objective	obtained	ongoing	outcomes	overseas
25. restricted	reinforced	resolution	restricted	registered	revealed

Exercise 91. Advanced (Academic Word List)

1. maintenance	manipulation	monitoring	nevertheless	maintenance	nonetheless
2. purchase	process	passive	positive	primary	purchase
3. data	deny	data	draft	bias	code
4. sought	sought	source	section	sphere	survive
5. resources	resolution	resources	responses	restraints	revolution
6. issue	image	impact	injury	insert	issue
7. equation	evolution	expansion	equation	exposure	evidence
8. minorities	mediation	migration	minimum	minorities	monitoring
9. section	sector	section	select	similar	solely
10. primary	passive	period	parallel	pursue	primary
11. traditional	techniques	traditional	transition	transport	temporary
12. adjustment	adjustment	ambiguous	anticipated	appropriate	assessment
13. economic	economic	eliminate	enhanced	evolution	financial
14. symbolic	sequence	somewhat	specific	specified	symbolic
15. chapter	chapter	chemical	clarity	clauses	capable
16. benefit	behalf	benefit	debate	denote	detect
17. period	period	parallel	passive	primary	pursue
18. aspects	abstract	access	aspects	adults	assume
19. labor	hence	tense	labor	trace	trend
20. involved	inferred	internal	invoked	involved	isolated
21. complex	coincide	collapse	complex	constant	comprise
22. aspects	abstract	access	adults	aspects	assume
23. occur	offset	option	output	access	occur
24. fundamental	fluctuations	forthcoming	framework	fundamental	furthermore
25. conduct	complex	coincide	conduct	constant	comprise

Exercise 92. Advanced (Academic Word List)

1. distribution	distribution	demonstrate	dimensions	diminished	discretion
2. procedure	procedure	preceding	predicted	prospect	protocol
3. response	relevant	required	research	response	retained
4. consistent	challenge	concurrent	confirmed	consistent	constraint
5. investigation	infrastructure	interpretation	investigation	integration	interaction
6. function	formats	formula	founded	function	finalizes
7. design	debate	denote	design	device	display
8. interpretation	infrastructure	interpretation	investigation	integration	interaction
9. substitution	subordinate	subsequent	substitution	successive	suspended
10. percent	percent	parallel	passive	primary	priority
11. available	arbitrary	assembly	assigned	authority	available
12. structure	structure	simulation	summary	statistics	strategy
13. elements	elements	enhanced	economic	empirical	enormous
14. individual	innovation	investment	identified	illustrated	individual
15. perceived	published	purchased	perceived	predicted	promoted
16. contract	context	concept	contrast	contract	contact
17. construction	concentration	conclusion	considerate	constitution	construction
18. distinction	depression	discretion	distinction	distortion	document
19. logic	label	labor	layer	legal	logic
20. draft	deny	draft	bias	code	data
21. similar	status	similar	survive	sustain	symbol
22. phase	panel	phase	policy	posed	prime
23. demonstrate	distribution	demonstrate	dimensions	diminished	discretion
24. monitoring	manipulation	nevertheless	maintenance	nonetheless	monitoring
25. community	commodity	conference	conference	community	controversy

Exercise 93. Advanced (Academic Word List)

1. acquisition	acquisition	adaptation	aggregate	allocation	alternative
2. formula	financial	flexibility	formula	founded	functional
3. analysis	accurate	analysis	arbitrary	attached	attitudes
4. indicate	indicate	inherent	instance	institute	integrity
5. financial	financial	flexibility	formula	founded	functional
6. maximum	marginal	maximum	mediation	migration	minimum
7. policy	posed	primary	pursue	policy	passive
8. technology	transmission	techniques	technology	termination	technical
9. concept	complex	collapse	constant	concept	contact
10. region	reveal	section	region	release	retain
11. license	likewise	lecture	liberal	license	federal
12. security	specific	stability	statistics	survive	security
13. final	factor	final	finite	focus	funds
14. identified	identified	illustrated	investment	innovation	integration
15. appropriate	adjustment	ambiguous	anticipated	appropriate	assessment
16. variables	variables	widespread	violation	virtually	voluntary
17. label	labor	label	layer	legal	logic
18. welfare	unique	volume	welfare	vehicle	version
19. discretion	distribution	demonstrate	dimensions	diminished	discretion
20. sustainable	subordinate	subsequent	substitution	successive	sustainable
21. create	civil	credit	create	chart	cited
22. annual	access	affect	albeit	annual	assume
23. conclusion	concentrate	conclusion	considerate	constitution	construction
24. assume	accurate	achieve	aspects	assure	assume
25. consumer	chemical	comprise	computer	corporate	consumer

Exercise 94. Advanced (Academic Word List)

1. factors	federal	formula	functions	factors	features
2. source	solely	sought	source	sphere	status
3. environment	enforcement	exploitation	established	environment	encountered
4. area	access	adult	area	alter	aid
5. immigration	immigration	implications	intelligence	intervention	innovation
6. reaction	reaction	research	resident	retained	revenue
7. physical	parallel	physical	potential	prospect	protocol
8. involved	inferred	internal	invoked	involved	isolated
9. principle	paragraph	perceived	persistent	predicted	principle
10. marginal	marginal	negative	nuclear	military	minimal
11. specific	security	statistics	survive	specific	stability
12. process	positive	primary	purchase	process	passive
13. potential	positive	potential	primary	priority	process
14. labor	hence	tense	labor	trace	trend
15. major	mature	media	norms	notion	major
16. retained	retained	revealed	required	rejected	removed
17. research	reaction	research	resident	retained	revenue
18. purchase	process	passive	positive	primary	purchase
19. investment	identified	illustrated	investment	innovation	integration
20. obtained	objective	obtained	ongoing	outcomes	overseas
21. constitutional	consequences	considerable	constitutional	construction	consultation
22. export	ethical	exhibit	expert	extract	export
23. whereas	version	volume	welfare	whereby	whereas
24. consultation	consideration	consultation	constitutional	construction	contribution
25. section	section	sector	select	similar	solely

Exercise 95. Advanced (Academic Word List)

1. core	chart	civil	code	core	cycle
2. cultural	complex	contract	contrary	contrast	cultural
3. scheme	scheme	section	similar	specific	structure
4. distribution	distribution	demonstrate	dimensions	diminished	discretion
5. affect	access	adults	affect	author	aware
6. region	reveal	section	retain	region	release
7. estimate	equation	estimate	evidence	exposure	external
8. computer	complex	computer	collapse	constant	comprise
9. impact	image	impact	income	initial	injury
10. mental	manual	mature	mental	method	mutual
11. area	access	adult	aid	alter	area
12. perceived	published	purchased	perceived	predicted	promoted
13. role	deny	role	bias	code	data
14. theory	target	thesis	topics	trendy	theory
15. technical	technical	temporary	thereby	transfer	transport
16. chapter	chapter	chemical	clarity	clauses	capable
17. evaluation	economic	equipment	equivalent	evaluation	expansion
18. structure	simulation	summary	structure	statistics	strategy
19. journal	granted	journal	parallel	potential	project
20. conflict	contact	context	concept	conduct	conflict
21. institute	indicate	inherent	instance	institute	integrity
22. resolution	resolution	resources	responses	restraints	revolution
23. analysis	accurate	arbitrary	analysis	attached	attitudes
24. sector	section	select	similar	solely	sector
25. equation	evolution	expansion	exposure	equation	evidence

Exercise 96. Advanced (Academic Word List)

1. adequate	academic	adequate	analogous	arbitrary	assistance
2. final	factor	final	finite	focus	funds
3. enforcement	enforcement	exploitation	established	environment	encountered
4. legislation	interaction	intervention	investment	justification	legislation
5. features	factors	features	federal	founded	functions
6. text	tapes	task	team	text	trace
7. focus	format	founded	function	funds	focus
8. administration	approximated	acknowledged	administration	approximated	automatically
9. evidence	enhance	equation	evidence	excluded	exposure
10. notion	normal	mature	notion	media	norms
11. response	relevant	required	research	response	retained
12. input	index	initial	injury	input	insert
13. constitutional	consequences	considerable	constitutional	construction	consultation
14. bond	data	deny	bond	brief	bulk
15. regulations	regulations	reinforced	resources	restraints	revolution
16. function	formats	formula	founded	finalizes	function
17. orientation	objective	obtained	ongoing	orientation	outcomes
18. strategies	strategies	statistics	simulation	summary	structures
19. volume	unique	volume	welfare	vehicle	version
20. context	context	contact	concept	conduct	conflict
21. stability	security	statistics	survive	specific	stability
22. issue	image	impact	injury	insert	issue
23. medical	medical	medium	method	military	network
24. authority	arbitrary	assembly	assigned	authority	available
25. subsequent	subordinate	subsequent	substitution	successive	suspended

Exercise 97. Advanced (Academic Word List)

1. formula	financial	flexibility	formula	founded	functional
2. appropriate	adjustment	ambiguous	anticipated	appropriate	assessment
3. circumstances	circumstances	compensation	consequences	constitutional	contemporary
4. assessment	assessment	alternative	ambiguous	amendment	analogous
5. maintenance	manipulation	monitoring	nevertheless	maintenance	nonetheless
6. participation	participation	phenomenon	practitioners	presumption	professional
7. principle	paragraph	principle	perceived	persistent	predicted
8. dimensions	distribution	demonstrate	dimensions	diminished	discretion
9. interpretation	infrastructure	interpretation	investigation	integration	interaction
10. concept	complex	collapse	constant	contact	concept
11. aspects	abstract	access	adults	assume	aspects
12. generation	guidelines	hypothesis	legislation	generation	illustrated
13. export	ethical	exhibit	expert	export	extract
14. transition	techniques	traditional	transition	transport	temporary
15. potential	positive	potential	primary	priority	process
16. impact	image	income	impact	initial	injury
17. trend	tapes	target	trend	topic	trace
18. issue	insert	impact	injury	image	issue
19. location	allocation	lecture	license	likewise	location
20. objective	objective	obtained	ongoing	outcomes	overseas
21. occur	offset	option	output	access	occur
22. capacity	capacity	channel	complex	confined	currency
23. purchase	process	purchase	passive	positive	primary
24. create	civil	cited	credit	create	chart
25. perspective	parameters	perspective	philosophy	preliminary	professional

Exercise 98. Advanced (Academic Word List)

1. data	bias	code	data	deny	draft
2. constraints	challenges	concurrent	confirmed	consistent	constraints
3. labor	hence	tense	labor	trace	trend
4. communication	comprehensive	concentration	consequences	communication	contemporary
5. indicate	indicate	inherent	instance	institute	integrity
6. consequences	consequences	considerable	constitutional	construction	consultation
7. promote	passive	positive	primary	process	promote
8. evolution	equation	evolution	expansion	exposure	evidence
9. styles	sought	sphere	status	styles	stress
10. available	arbitrary	assembly	assigned	available	authority
11. intelligence	immigration	implications	intelligence	intervention	innovation
12. fees	bias	fees	files	focus	funds
13. journal	journal	granted	parallel	potential	project
14. normal	mutual	neutral	normal	notion	nuclear
15. flexibility	facilitate	financial	foundation	flexibility	framework
16. source	solely	sought	source	sphere	status
17. elements	elements	enhanced	economic	empirical	enormous
18. clause	clarity	clause	couple	criteria	crucial
19. period	primary	pursue	parallel	period	passive
20. enhanced	elements	enhanced	economic	empirical	enormous
21. revenue	reaction	research	resident	retained	revenue
22. income	implicit	income	indicate	induced	integral
23. recovery	recovery	relevant	reluctant	removed	response
24. injury	image	impact	income	initial	injury
25. expansion	economic	equipment	equivalent	evaluation	expansion

Exercise 99. Advanced (Academic Word List)

1. constitutional	consequences	considerable	constitutional	construction	consultation
2. financial	financial	flexibility	formula	founded	functional
3. method	medical	medium	method	military	network
4. definition	definition	deduction	distortion	distinction	document
5. illustrated	innovation	investment	identified	individual	illustrated
6. obtained	objective	obtained	ongoing	outcomes	overseas
7. individual	innovation	investment	identified	illustrated	individual
8. resources	resolution	resources	responses	restraints	revolution
9. required	retained	revealed	required	rejected	removed
10. community	commodity	conference	conference	community	controversy
11. contract	context	concept	contrast	contact	contract
12. text	tapes	task	team	text	trace
13. sufficient	strategies	submitted	subsidiary	sufficient	suspended
14. interval	inferred	inherent	integral	internal	interval
15. specific	security	statistics	survive	specific	stability
16. estimate	estimate	equation	evidence	exposure	external
17. traditional	techniques	traditional	transition	transport	temporary
18. perceived	published	purchased	perceived	predicted	promoted
19. percent	percent	parallel	passive	primary	priority
20. institute	indicate	inherent	instance	institute	integrity
21. commitment	components	commenced	commission	constitution	commitment
22. assume	assume	accurate	achieve	aspects	assure
23. minimum	marginal	minimize	minimum	military	minimal
24. sector	section	sector	select	similar	solely
25. previous	potential	previous	promote	prospect	protocol

Exercise 100. Advanced (Academic Word List)

1. communication	comprehensive	concentration	consequences	communication	contemporary
2. evaluation	economic	equipment	evaluation	equivalent	expansion
3. environment	enforcement	exploitation	established	environment	encountered
4. analysis	arbitrary	attached	attitudes	accurate	analysis
5. process	process	passive	positive	primary	purchase
6. section	sector	select	section	similar	solely
7. cultural	complex	contract	contrary	contrast	cultural
8. published	perceived	predicted	promoted	published	purchased
9. identified	identified	illustrated	investment	innovation	integration
10. similar	status	similar	survive	sustain	symbol
11. investment	identified	illustrated	investment	innovation	integration
12. regulations	regulations	reinforced	resources	restraints	revolution
13. final	factor	final	finite	focus	funds
14. definition	definition	deduction	distortion	distinction	document
15. major	mature	media	norms	notion	major
16. export	ethical	exhibit	expert	export	extract
17. aspects	abstract	access	aspects	adults	assume
18. benefit	behalf	benefit	debate	denote	detect
19. distinction	depression	discretion	distinction	distortion	document
20. principle	principle	paragraph	perceived	persistent	predicted
21. impact	image	initial	injury	impact	income
22. consumer	chemical	comprise	computer	corporate	consumer
23. potential	positive	potential	primary	priority	process
24. area	access	adult	aid	alter	area
25. variables	widespread	variables	violation	virtually	voluntary

Progress Charts

Progress Charts

Directions: Write the exercise you are doing in the top row.

1. Find your score in the left column. (Remember: Your
   score is the number of correct answers *minus* any
   mistakes.)
2. Place a dot (•) where the two lines meet.
3. After you do another exercise, connect the dots.

Examples:
Exercise 87: 24 correct, 1 mistake (= 23)
Exercise 73: 25 correct, 1 mistake (= 24)
Exercise 82: 23 correct, 2 mistakes (= 21)
Exercise 79: 23 correct, 0 mistakes (= 23)

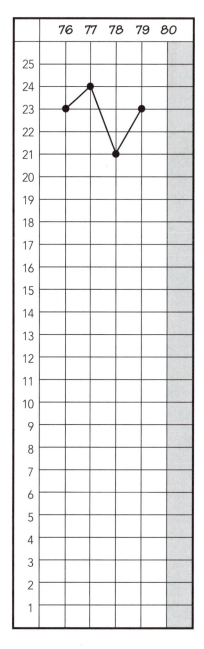

Name _____

Timed Word Selection Rate Chart

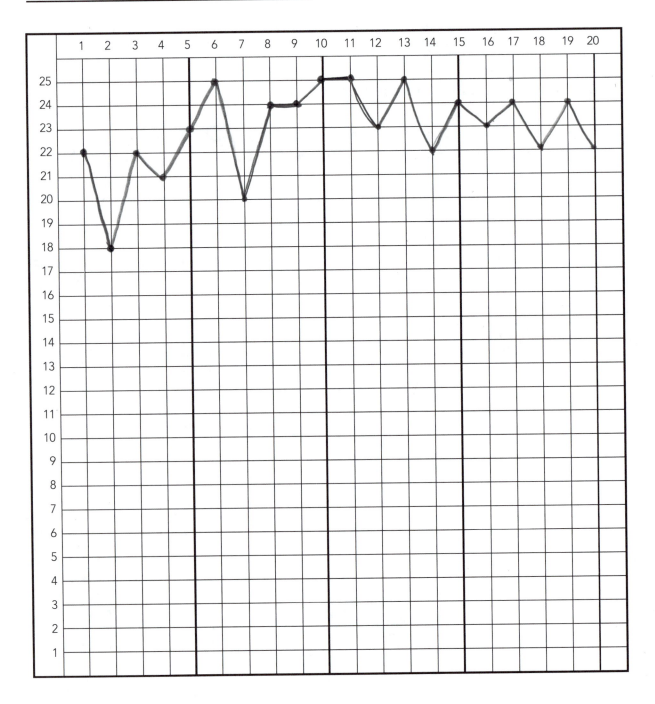

Name _____

Timed Word Selection Rate Chart

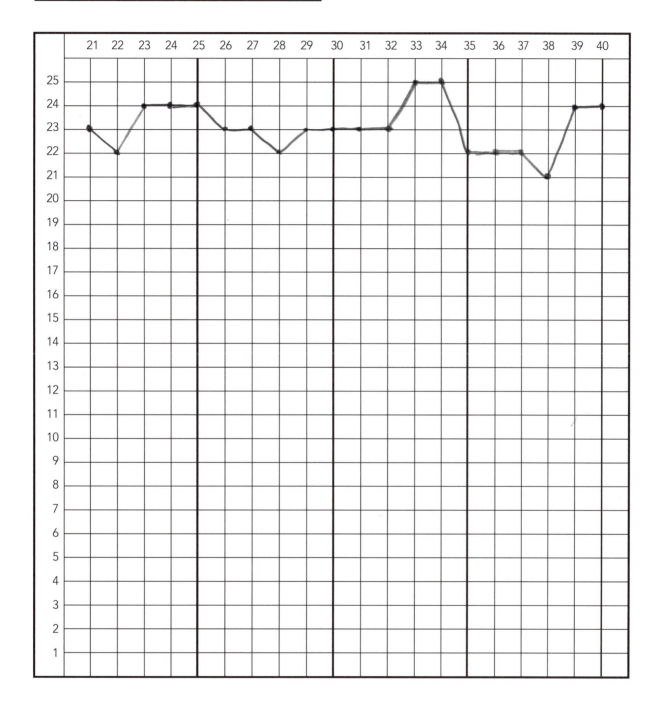

Name _____

Timed Word Selection Rate Chart

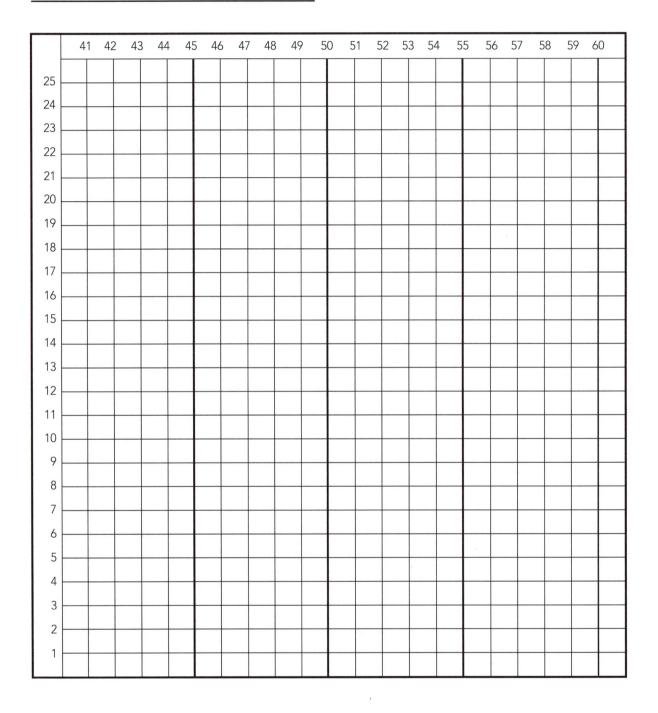

Name _____

Timed Word Selection Rate Chart

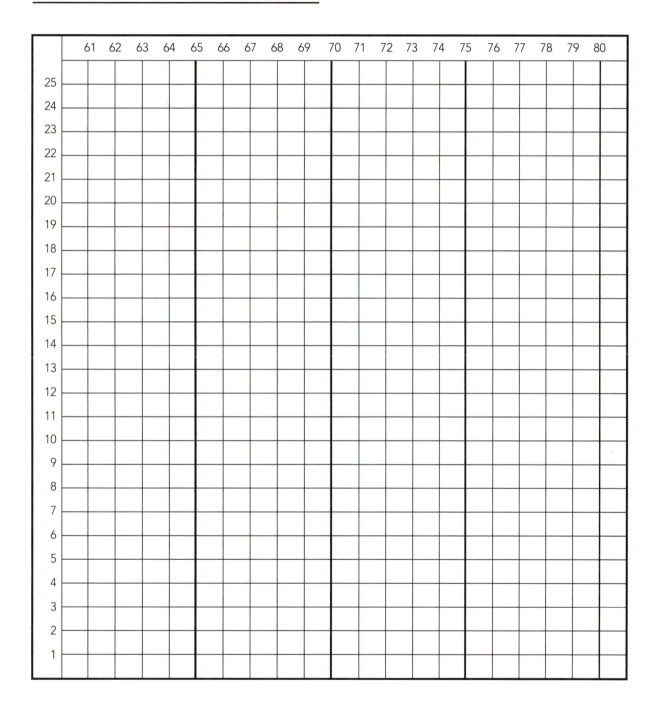

Name _____

Timed Word Selection Rate Chart

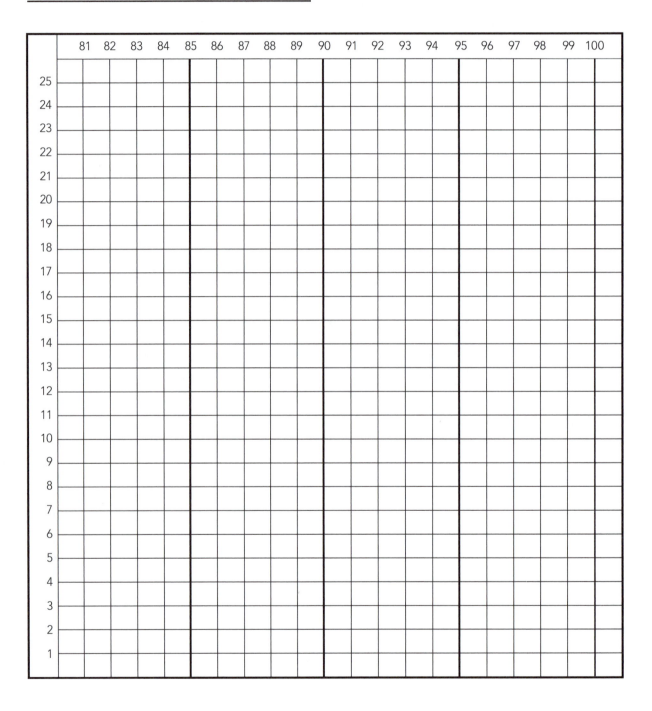